TRIPLE · TESTED · FOR YOUR SUCCESS EVERY TIME

For more than 50 years, *The Australian Women's Weekly* Test Kitchen has been creating marvellous recipes that come with a guarantee of success. First, the recipes always work — just follow the instructions and you, too, will get the results you see in the photographs. Second, and perhaps more importantly, they are delicious — created by experienced home economists and chefs, all triple-tested and, thanks to their straightforward instructions, easy to make.

Note
All the recipes have been analysed for their
fat content and kilojoule count per serving.
The analyses are based on Australian
ingredients and assume that:
• meat was lean and trimmed of all visible fat
• skin was removed from chicken
• only the exact amount of oil, butter or
  margarine specified in the recipe was used
• oil spray was included as 3 grams of fat
• dairy products with the lowest-fat content
  were used.

British and North American readers:
Please note that Australian cup and spoon
measurements are metric.
A quick conversion guide appears
on page 119.

We've kept fats down and flavours up in this delicious book that's right at the front of nutrition guidelines. Counting fats grams is as easy as checking the note at the end of each recipe, so you can keep tabs on just what you are eating. If you have diabetes, many of our recipes will fit well into your lifestyle.

There are ideas for guilt-free snacks, light and fresh main meals drawing on cuisines from around the world, scrumptious accompaniments and wonderfully inventive desserts that won't break your kilojoule bank! Mix and match the recipes from each section to create a dinner party menu which will surprise and delight your guests.

First, though, turn to page 112 for the low-down on low-fat eating, and why it's important to you, then choose a tempting recipe or two and just see how easy it is!

Pamela Clark

FOOD EDITOR

contents

lunches and snacks

Healthy and delicious, our snacks, lunches and soups are a great way to kick off your next-to-no-fat lifestyle. We've given you a fantastic variety for any occasion — all easy, and so tasty that no-one will miss the fat. Always be sure to check the labels when you are shopping, and use low-fat and low-salt products throughout, as we did.

spicy seafood bouillabaisse

PREPARATION TIME 40 MINUTES • COOKING TIME 30 MINUTES

**500g boneless white
  fish fillets**
300g medium uncooked prawns
16 small (230g) mussels
1/2 teaspoon olive oil
**4 medium (520g) tomatoes,
  peeled, chopped roughly**
**1 large (300g) red Spanish
  onion, sliced**
2 cloves garlic, crushed
**2 small fresh red chillies,
  chopped finely**
1/3 cup (65g) basmati rice
10cm strip orange rind
2 cups (500ml) fish stock
2 cups (500ml) water
1 cup (250ml) dry white wine
pinch saffron powder
**1 tablespoon chopped
  fresh dill**

1 Cut fish into 5cm pieces. Shell and devein prawns, leaving heads and tails intact. Scrub mussels, remove beards.

2 Heat oil in large pan, add tomatoes, onion, garlic and chillies, cook, stirring, about 5 minutes or until onion is soft.

3 Add rice, rind, stock, water, wine and saffron, boil, uncovered, about 10 minutes or until rice is tender, stirring occasionally.

4 Add fish and prawns, simmer, uncovered, about 3 minutes or until seafood is almost tender. Add mussels and dill, cook, covered, about 2 minutes or until mussels open. Discard orange rind.

SERVES 6

Recipe best made just before serving

Freeze Not suitable
Microwave Suitable

Diabetic Additional carbohydrate required
Per serve fat 3.9g; 1040kJ

caesar salad with prosciutto and potatoes

PREPARATION TIME 20 MINUTES • COOKING TIME 20 MINUTES

4 slices (60g) prosciutto

3 slices rye bread

cooking-oil spray

3 medium (600g) potatoes

45g can anchovy fillets, rinsed, drained

1 large cos lettuce

1 tablespoon grated parmesan cheese

DRESSING

1 teaspoon Dijon mustard

2 cloves garlic, crushed

2 tablespoons grated parmesan cheese

3/4 cup (180ml) low-fat yogurt

1/3 cup fresh basil leaves

1 Grill prosciutto until crisp, break into pieces. Coat bread with cooking-oil spray, grill on both sides until crisp. Cut bread into 1cm cubes.

2 Boil, steam or microwave unpeeled potatoes until just tender; drain, rinse under cold water, drain. Cut potatoes into 1cm slices.

3 Press anchovies with absorbent paper to remove excess oil.

4 Reserve 8 lettuce leaves, tear remaining lettuce into pieces.

5 Combine lettuce, potato, bread cubes, half the prosciutto and half the cheese in large bowl; mix gently.

6 Line salad bowl with reserved lettuce leaves, top with salad mixture and remaining prosciutto, cheese and half the anchovies. Drizzle with dressing.

Dressing Blend remaining anchovies, mustard, garlic and cheese until finely chopped. Add yogurt and basil, blend until basil is chopped coarsely.

SERVES 4

Dressing can be made a day ahead; assemble salad just before serving

Storage Covered, in refrigerator
Freeze Not suitable
Microwave Potatoes suitable

Diabetic Suitable
Per serve fat 4.5g; 940kJ

thai-style stir-fried prawn salad

PREPARATION TIME 35 MINUTES • COOKING TIME 15 MINUTES

500g uncooked medium prawns

1 clove garlic, crushed

2 tablespoons lime juice

1 tablespoon mild sweet
chilli sauce

1¹/₂ teaspoons fish sauce

1 tablespoon chopped fresh
coriander leaves

1 tablespoon chopped fresh
lemon grass

250g asparagus

1 tablespoon peanut oil

500g baby bok choy, chopped

1 medium (200g) yellow
capsicum, chopped

1 cup (80g) snow pea sprouts

1 tablespoon shredded fresh
basil leaves

1 Shell and devein prawns, leaving tails intact. Combine prawns, garlic, 1 tablespoon of the juice, chilli sauce, ¹/₂ teaspoon of the fish sauce, coriander and lemon grass in bowl; mix well. Cover, refrigerate several hours or overnight.

2 Drain prawns; discard marinade. Cut asparagus into 5cm lengths. Add asparagus to large pan of boiling water, drain immediately, rinse under cold water; drain.

3 Heat oil in wok or large pan, add prawns, stir-fry until prawns are tender, remove from wok. Add asparagus, bok choy and capsicum to wok or pan, stir-fry until just tender. Add remaining juice, remaining fish sauce, sprouts and basil, stir-fry until sprouts are just wilted. Serve vegetables topped with prawns.

SERVES 4

Marinade can be prepared a day
ahead; stir-fry just before serving

Storage Covered, in refrigerator
Freeze Not suitable
Microwave Asparagus suitable

Diabetic Additional carbohydrate required
Per serve fat 6.1g; 630kJ

lamb satay

PREPARATION TIME 30 MINUTES • COOKING TIME 20 MINUTES

Soak skewers in water for several hours or overnight to prevent them from burning.

500g lean lamb fillets

3 cloves garlic, crushed

2 teaspoons fish sauce

**2 tablespoons mild sweet
    chilli sauce**

**2 teaspoons grated
    fresh ginger**

1/4 cup (60ml) lime juice

**2 tablespoons low-salt
    crunchy peanut butter**

1 teaspoon ground cumin

1 teaspoon ground turmeric

cooking-oil spray

SAUCE

1/4 cup (60ml) white vinegar

**2 tablespoons sugar or
    powdered artificial
    sweetener**

**1 tablespoon mild sweet
    chilli sauce**

**1 tablespoon chopped
    unsalted roasted peanuts**

**1 tablespoon chopped fresh
    coriander leaves**

1 Cut fillets in half lengthways,
   then cut into thin strips.
   Combine lamb, garlic, sauces,
   ginger, juice, peanut butter and
   spices in bowl; mix well. Cover;
   refrigerate 1 hour.

2 Thread lamb onto 12 small
   skewers.

3 Coat hot griddle pan with
   cooking-oil spray, add skewers,
   cook until lamb is tender. Serve
   with sauce.

Sauce Combine vinegar and sugar
in small pan, stir over heat until
sugar is dissolved, boil, uncovered,
2 minutes. Stir in remaining
ingredients.

SERVES 4

Recipe can be prepared a day ahead

Storage Covered, in refrigerator
Freeze Uncooked recipe suitable
Microwave Not suitable

Diabetic Suitable for occasional use;
additional carbohydrate is required
Per serve fat 12.4g; 1055kJ

thai pork and corn cakes

PREPARATION TIME 30 MINUTES • COOKING TIME 25 MINUTES

500g lean pork and veal mince

1 tablespoon red curry paste

1 egg, beaten lightly

6 green onions, chopped finely

130g can corn kernels, drained

1/2 cup (35g) stale wholemeal breadcrumbs

1/4 cup chopped fresh coriander leaves

DIPPING SAUCE

1/2 cup (125ml) mild sweet chilli sauce

1/2 small (65g) green cucumber, chopped finely

1 Combine all ingredients in bowl. Roll rounded tablespoons of mixture into balls, shape into patties, place on oven tray.

2 Bake, uncovered, in hot oven about 25 minutes or until browned, turn halfway during cooking. Serve with dipping sauce.

Dipping sauce Combine ingredients in small bowl.

MAKES 16

Recipe can be prepared a day ahead

Storage Covered, in refrigerator
Freeze Uncooked patties suitable
Microwave Not suitable

Diabetic Additional carbohydrate required
Per serve (one cake) fat 3.7g; 345kJ

beef salad with garlic dressing

PREPARATION TIME 25 MINUTES • COOKING TIME 60 MINUTES

**500g piece lean beef
   rump steak**
**1 teaspoon cracked
   black pepper**
2 tablespoons red wine vinegar
**2 teaspoons chopped
   fresh thyme**
2 teaspoons seeded mustard
cooking-oil spray
1 medium butter lettuce
**1 cup (50g) firmly packed fresh
   watercress sprigs**
250g cherry tomatoes, halved
**1 small (130g) green
   cucumber, sliced**
**1 small (100g) red Spanish
   onion, sliced**

GARLIC DRESSING

3 medium (210g) bulbs garlic
1 teaspoon balsamic vinegar
1/2 cup (125ml) chicken stock
**2 tablespoons low-fat
   sour cream**

1 Combine beef, pepper, vinegar, thyme and mustard in bowl, cover; refrigerate overnight.

2 Coat griddle pan with cooking-oil spray, add beef, cook until well browned on both sides and tender. Stand beef 5 minutes before slicing thinly.

3 Serve beef on lettuce leaves with remaining ingredients; drizzle with garlic dressing.

Garlic dressing Place whole unpeeled garlic bulbs in small baking dish, coat with cooking oil spray, bake, uncovered, in moderate oven about 50 minutes or until bulbs are soft; wrap in foil, cool. Squeeze garlic from cloves. You need 2 tablespoons of garlic puree for this recipe. Blend or process garlic, vinegar, stock and cream until smooth.

SERVES 4

Dressing can be made a day ahead

Storage Covered, in refrigerator
Freeze Not suitable
Microwave Not suitable

Diabetic Additional carbohydrate required
Per serve fat 8.3g; 1005kJ

cajun chicken with mango chilli

PREPARATION TIME 15 MINUTES • COOKING TIME 15 MINUTES

**500g skinless chicken
   breast fillets**
1 teaspoon cayenne pepper
1/2 teaspoon cumin seeds
1/2 teaspoon dried oregano
**1/2 teaspoon dried
   thyme leaves**
1 teaspoon garlic salt
cooking-oil spray
200g mixed salad leaves
**2 medium (150g) egg
   tomatoes, sliced**

MANGO CHILLI DRESSING

**1 medium (430g) mango,
   chopped**
1 small fresh red chilli, chopped
1/2 teaspoon grated lime rind
1/4 cup (60ml) lime juice
1/2 teaspoon sugar

1 Coat chicken in combined pepper, seeds, herbs and salt. Heat griddle pan, coat with cooking-oil spray, add chicken, cook until browned on both sides and tender, cool. Slice chicken diagonally.

2 Place salad leaves in bowl, top with chicken and tomatoes; drizzle with mango chilli dressing.

Mango chilli dressing Blend or process all ingredients until smooth.

SERVES 4

Recipe can be prepared several hours ahead

Storage Covered, separately, in refrigerator
Freeze Not suitable
Microwave Not suitable

Diabetic Additional carbohydrate required
Per serve fat 3.8g; 815kJ

cajun chicken with mango chilli *(front)*
beef salad with garlic dressing *(back)*

kumara, leek and sage frittata

PREPARATION TIME 20 MINUTES • COOKING TIME 50 MINUTES

cooking-oil spray

2 medium (800g) kumara

1 small (200g) leek, sliced

1 clove garlic, crushed

1 tablespoon chopped fresh sage leaves

3 eggs

3 egg whites

1/2 cup (125ml) low-fat milk

1/3 cup (40g) grated low-fat cheddar cheese

1 tablespoon chopped fresh parsley

1 Coat 25cm round flan dish (1.5 litre/6 cup) with cooking-oil spray. Cut kumara into 5mm slices. Boil, steam or microwave kumara until tender; drain.

2 Heat non-stick pan, coat with cooking-oil spray, add leek and garlic, cook, covered, over low heat until leek is tender, stirring occasionally. Stir in half the sage.

3 Place half the kumara over base of prepared dish, top with leek mixture, then remaining kumara. Pour combined eggs, egg whites, milk, cheese and parsley over kumara, sprinkle with remaining sage. Bake, uncovered, in moderate oven about 35 minutes or until frittata is firm.

SERVES 6

Recipe can be made a day ahead

Storage Covered, in refrigerator
Freeze Not suitable
Microwave Kumara and leek suitable

Diabetic Suitable
Per serve fat 4.9g; 730kJ

curried lamb pasties

PREPARATION TIME 45 MINUTES • COOKING TIME 40 MINUTES

**2 cups (300g) white
plain flour**
**1 cup (160g) wholemeal
plain flour**
1/3 cup (55g) polenta
1 tablespoon cumin seeds
125g low-fat cream cheese
**3/4 cup (180ml) warm
water, approximately**
low-fat milk
cooking-oil spray

FILLING

**250g very lean
minced lamb**
**1/2 small (80g) red
capsicum, chopped finely**
**1/2 small (125g) kumara,
grated coarsely**
**1 small (80g) onion,
chopped finely**
**2 teaspoons green
curry paste**
1/4 cup (60ml) beef stock
1/3 cup (40g) frozen peas
**1 tablespoon chopped fresh
mint leaves**

1 Sift flours into bowl, add polenta and seeds. Rub in cheese (or process flours, polenta, seeds and cheese until combined). Add enough water to make ingredients cling together.

2 Press dough into a ball, knead gently on floured surface until smooth. Wrap in plastic, refrigerate 30 minutes.

3 Roll half the pastry between sheets of baking paper until 2mm thick. Cut pastry into 6 rounds (12cm diameter).

Repeat with remaining pastry. Place rounded tablespoons of cold filling in centre of each round. Brush edges with a little milk, fold in half, press edges together to seal.

4 Place pasties on oven tray which has been coated with cooking-oil spray, brush pasties with a little extra milk.

5 Bake, uncovered, in moderately hot oven about 25 minutes or until browned.

Filling Heat non-stick pan, add lamb; cook, stirring, until browned, remove from pan. Reheat pan, coat with cooking-oil spray, add capsicum, kumara and onion; cook, stirring, until vegetables are soft.

Return lamb to pan, add curry paste; cook, stirring, until fragrant. Add stock and peas; cook, stirring, 3 minutes or until liquid has evaporated. Stir in mint; cool.

MAKES 12

Pasties can be made a day ahead

Storage Covered, in refrigerator
Freeze Cooked pasties suitable
Microwave Filling suitable

Diabetic Suitable
Per pasty fat 4.4g; 855kJ

seafood spring rolls with sweet chilli sauce

PREPARATION TIME 40 MINUTES • COOKING TIME 15 MINUTES

2 teaspoons vegetable oil

200g scallops

2 green onions, chopped

1 clove garlic, crushed

1 small (150g) bok choy, chopped

250g medium cooked prawns, shelled, chopped

1/4 cup (60ml) mild sweet chilli sauce

1 teaspoon fish sauce

1 tablespoon chopped fresh coriander leaves

12 rice paper rounds (22cm)

1 Heat half the oil in pan, add scallops, onions and garlic, cook, stirring, until scallops are just tender; remove from pan. Heat remaining oil in pan, add bok choy, cook, stirring, until wilted.

2 Combine scallop mixture in bowl with bok choy, prawns, 1 tablespoon of the chilli sauce, fish sauce and coriander, mix well; cool. Drain seafood mixture; reserve liquid.

3 Dip rice paper rounds, 1 at a time, in hot water until softened. Place about 1 tablespoon of seafood mixture in centre of rounds, roll to enclose filling. Bring reserved liquid to boil in pan, add remaining chilli sauce; serve mixture as a dipping sauce.

SERVES 4

Recipe best made just before serving

Freeze Not suitable
Microwave Not suitable

Diabetic Suitable
Per serve fat 3.4g; 405kJ

ginger vegetable gow gees with dipping sauce

PREPARATION TIME 1 HOUR • COOKING TIME 30 MINUTES

cooking-oil spray

1 small (150g) red
   capsicum, chopped

1 small (250g) kumara, grated

1 small (150g) bok choy,
   chopped finely

2 green onions, chopped finely

2 teaspoons grated
   fresh ginger

1 clove garlic, crushed

1 cup (80g) bean
   sprouts, chopped

1 tablespoon chopped fresh
   mint leaves

40 gow gee wrappers

DIPPING SAUCE

1 tablespoon low-salt
   soy sauce

2 teaspoons lime juice

2 teaspoons sugar

1/4 teaspoon sambal oelek

1 Coat non-stick pan with
   cooking-oil spray, add capsicum,
   kumara, bok choy, onions,
   ginger and garlic, cook, stirring,
   until vegetables are just tender.
   Stir in sprouts and mint.

2 Place a rounded teaspoon of
   mixture on centre of each
   wrapper. Brush edges with
   water, gather together in centre,
   press firmly to seal.

3 Place gow gees in single layer in
   steamer, cook, covered, over
   simmering water for 20 minutes.
   Serve with dipping sauce.

Dipping sauce Combine all
ingredients in bowl; mix well.

MAKES 40

*Gow gees and sauce can be
prepared 3 hours ahead*

Storage Covered, separately,
in refrigerator
Freeze Not suitable
Microwave Vegetable mixture
suitable

Diabetic Suitable
Per gow gee fat 0g; 20kJ

salmon dip with crispitas

PREPARATION TIME 15 MINUTES • COOKING TIME 8 MINUTES

210g can salmon,
  drained, flaked
150g low-fat ricotta cheese
1/2 cup (125ml) low-fat
  yogurt
1 small (80g) onion, chopped
1 teaspoon drained green
  peppercorns
2 tablespoons chopped
  fresh dill
400g packet wholemeal
  pitta bread
cooking-oil spray
3 teaspoons Cajun seasoning

1 Process salmon, cheese, yogurt, onion, peppercorns and dill until just combined. Split each pitta bread in half, coat with cooking-oil spray, sprinkle with seasoning. Cut each pitta bread into 10 triangles, place on oven tray.

2 Bake, uncovered, in moderate oven about 8 minutes or until bread is crisp. Serve with salmon dip.

SERVES 10

Recipe can be made a day ahead

Storage Dip, covered, in refrigerator. Crispitas, in airtight container
Freeze Not suitable
Microwave Not suitable

Diabetic Suitable
Per serve fat 4.8g; 735kJ

wholemeal kumara pretzels

PREPARATION TIME 1 HOUR • COOKING TIME 40 MINUTES

2 cups (300g) white
   plain flour
1¹/₃ cups (210g) wholemeal
   plain flour
160g uncooked kumara,
   grated coarsely
2 teaspoons (7g) dried yeast
1 teaspoon sugar
1 teaspoon salt
2 tablespoons chopped
   fresh chives
1 tablespoon chopped
   fresh oregano
1 clove garlic, crushed
²/₃ cup (160ml) low-fat milk
2 teaspoons vegetable oil
²/₃ cup (160ml) warm
   water, approximately
cooking-oil spray
1 egg, beaten lightly
poppy seeds
fine sea salt

1 Sift flours into large bowl, add kumara, yeast, sugar, salt, chives, oregano and garlic; mix well. Stir in combined milk, oil and enough water to mix to a soft dough.

2 Turn dough onto floured surface, knead about 5 minutes or until dough is elastic. Divide dough into 12 portions, roll each portion with fingers, on floured surface, to 60cm length, tapering dough at both ends.

3 Shape dough into pretzels by first forming a loop, then twisting and folding the 2 ends over the loop. Place pretzels about 5cm apart on oven trays which have been coated with cooking-oil spray, cover; stand in warm place about 10 minutes.

4 Add pretzels in batches to large pan of boiling water for about 30 seconds, remove when pretzels rise to surface. Place pretzels in single layer on oven trays, cool 10 minutes or until dry. Brush pretzels with egg, sprinkle lightly with seeds and sea salt.

5 Bake pretzels in hot oven about 25 minutes, cool on trays.

MAKES 12

Pretzels can be made a day ahead

Storage Airtight container
Freeze Suitable
Microwave Not suitable

Diabetic Suitable
Per pretzel fat 2g; 690kJ

Shape pretzel loop and twist

Fold ends over loop and twist

grilled vegetable salad with creamy dressing

PREPARATION TIME 35 MINUTES (PLUS STANDING TIME) • COOKING TIME 30 MINUTES

2 medium (400g) potatoes

1 large (500g) kumara

200g medium flat mushrooms

cooking-oil spray

1 teaspoon Cajun seasoning

250g English spinach

**1 medium green oak
   leaf lettuce**

CREAMY DRESSING

**1/4 cup (15g) sun-dried
   tomatoes without oil**

1/2 cup (125ml) low-fat milk

**1/2 cup (125ml) low-fat
   sour cream**

**2 teaspoons chopped
   fresh oregano**

1 clove garlic, crushed

2 teaspoons balsamic vinegar

1 Cut potatoes and kumara into
   1cm slices. Boil, steam or
   microwave potatoes and kumara
   until just tender; pat dry with
   absorbent paper.

2 Coat potatoes, kumara and
   mushrooms with cooking-oil
   spray; sprinkle with seasoning.

3 Cook vegetables in batches
   on hot griddle pan until
   browned and tender, serve
   with torn spinach and lettuce
   leaves; drizzle with creamy
   dressing.

   Creamy dressing Cover
   tomatoes with boiling water
   in small heatproof bowl, stand
   20 minutes or until soft. Drain
   tomatoes, chop finely.

Whisk milk and sour cream in
bowl, stir in tomatoes, oregano
and garlic; whisk in vinegar.

SERVES 4

*Recipe best made just before
serving*

Freeze Not suitable
Microwave Potatoes and kumara
suitable

Diabetic Suitable
Per serve fat 6.7g; 1030kJ

roasted eggplants with capsicum and pesto

PREPARATION TIME 50 MINUTES (PLUS MARINATING TIME) • COOKING TIME 40 MINUTES

1 large (350g) red capsicum
14 (840g) finger eggplants
coarse cooking salt
4 slices wholemeal bread
2 tablespoons flaked parmesan cheese

MARINADE

1/3 cup (80ml) lemon juice
1 tablespoon balsamic vinegar
3 teaspoons mild sweet chilli sauce
2 teaspoons sugar
2 cloves garlic, crushed
2 teaspoons olive oil

PESTO

1 1/2 cups loosely packed basil leaves
2 tablespoons fresh oregano
2/3 cup (130g) low-fat ricotta cheese
2 tablespoons water

1 Quarter capsicum, remove seeds and membranes. Grill capsicum, skin-side up, until skin blisters and blackens. Peel skin, slice capsicum. Cut eggplants into 4 slices lengthways, sprinkle with salt, stand 20 minutes.

2 Rinse eggplants; drain, pat dry with absorbent paper. Combine eggplants and marinade in bowl, cover, refrigerate 30 minutes.

3 Drain eggplants, reserve marinade. Remove crusts from bread, toast bread. Grill eggplant slices on both sides until tender, brushing with some of the reserved marinade.

4 Place toast on serving plates, top with eggplants, capsicum, cheese and pesto.

Marinade Combine all ingredients in bowl; mix well.

Pesto Blend or process all ingredients and 1/4 cup (60ml) of reserved marinade until smooth.

SERVES 4

Pesto can be made 2 days ahead

Storage Covered, in refrigerator
Freeze Not suitable
Microwave Not suitable

Diabetic Suitable
Per serve fat 7.4g; 535kJ

vegetarian pizzas with pepita pesto

PREPARATION TIME 50 MINUTES (PLUS STANDING TIME) • COOKING TIME 25 MINUTES

1/2 cup (75g) pepitas
1/4 cup firmly packed fresh
 basil leaves
1/4 cup firmly packed fresh
 parsley sprigs
1 clove garlic, crushed
1/4 cup (60ml) tomato puree
1 small (300g) kumara
cooking-oil spray
150g button mushrooms, sliced
1/2 cup (60g) grated low-fat
 cheddar cheese
1/2 cup (50g) grated low-fat
 mozzarella cheese
1/2 cup (40g) grated
 parmesan cheese

PIZZA DOUGH

2 teaspoons (7g) dried yeast
1 teaspoon sugar
1/4 cup (60ml) warm water
11/2 cups (240g) wholemeal
 plain flour
1/2 teaspoon salt
1/3 cup (80ml) warm
 low-fat milk
2 teaspoons olive oil

1 Add pepitas to dry pan, cook, stirring, over low heat about 5 minutes or until pepitas have popped; cool.

2 Process pepitas, herbs and garlic until combined. Gradually add puree while motor is operating.

3 Using a vegetable peeler, cut kumara into ribbons. Divide pizza dough into 4 portions. Roll each portion on floured surface to 15cm round, place on oven trays which have been coated with cooking-oil spray.

4 Divide pepita pesto between pizzas, top with kumara and mushrooms, sprinkle with combined cheeses. Bake in moderately hot oven about 20 minutes or until browned and crisp.

Pizza dough Combine yeast and sugar in small bowl, stir in water, cover; stand in warm place about 10 minutes or until mixture is frothy. Sift flour and salt into large bowl, stir in yeast mixture, milk and oil, mix to a firm dough. Turn dough onto floured surface, knead about 5 minutes or until dough is smooth and elastic. Place dough in bowl sprayed with cooking oil spray, cover, stand in warm place about 30 minutes or until doubled in size.

SERVES 4

Recipe best made just before serving

Freeze Suitable
Microwave Not suitable

Diabetic Suitable for occasional use
Per serve fat 13.1g; 1655kJ

tomato, bean and pasta soup

PREPARATION TIME 20 MINUTES • COOKING TIME 35 MINUTES

3/4 cup (135g) wholemeal
   pasta spirals
1 large (200g) onion,
   chopped
1 litre (4 cups) chicken stock
500ml jar tomato pasta sauce
1 teaspoon chopped
   fresh oregano
440g can four-bean mix,
   rinsed, drained
2 medium (240g) zucchini,
   chopped coarsely
2 tablespoons chopped
   fresh parsley

1 Add pasta gradually to large pan of boiling water, boil, uncovered, until just tender; drain well.

2 Combine onion and 2 tablespoons of the stock in large pan, stir over heat until onion is soft. Add remaining stock, sauce and oregano, boil, uncovered, 15 minutes.

3 Add beans and zucchini, cook, uncovered, 10 minutes. Add pasta and parsley, stir until hot.

SERVES 4

Recipe can be made a day ahead

Storage Covered, in refrigerator
Freeze Suitable
Microwave Pasta suitable

Diabetic Suitable
Per serve fat 1.6g; 850kJ

ginger tofu and vegetable stir-fry

PREPARATION TIME 15 MINUTES • COOKING TIME 10 MINUTES

3 Chinese dried mushrooms

1 medium (120g) carrot

1 medium (200g) yellow capsicum

375g packet firm tofu, drained

2 teaspoons peanut oil

1 teaspoon sesame oil

2 teaspoons finely grated fresh ginger

2 cloves garlic, crushed

1 cup (80g) bean sprouts

1/2 bunch (250g) baby bok choy, shredded

1/3 cup (60g) drained water chestnuts, sliced

2 tablespoons oyster sauce

2 teaspoons cornflour

1 tablespoon water

6 lettuce leaves

1 Place mushrooms in heatproof bowl, cover with boiling water, stand 20 minutes; drain, discard liquid and stems, slice caps.

2 Cut carrot and capsicum into long thin strips. Cut tofu into 1cm cubes.

3 Heat oils in wok or frying pan, add ginger and garlic, stir-fry 1 minute. Add carrot and capsicum, stir-fry until vegetables are just tender.

4 Add mushrooms, sprouts, bok choy, chestnuts, oyster sauce and blended cornflour and water, cook, stirring, until sauce boils and thickens; stir in tofu. Serve in trimmed lettuce leaves.

SERVES 6

Recipe best made just before serving

Freeze Not suitable
Microwave Suitable

Diabetic Additional carbohydrate required
Per serve fat 8g; 470kJ

jalapeño chilli cornbread

PREPARATION TIME 10 MINUTES • COOKING TIME 45 MINUTES

cooking-oil spray

2 cups (300g) self-raising flour

1 teaspoon baking powder

1 tablespoon sugar

1¼ cups (210g) polenta

1 egg, lightly beaten

¾ cup (180ml) buttermilk

¾ cup (180ml) low-fat milk

130g can corn kernels, rinsed, drained

2 small fresh red chillies, chopped

2 teaspoons chopped drained jalapeño chillies

2 teaspoons polenta, extra

1 Coat 20cm ring pan with cooking-oil spray. Combine sifted flour, baking powder and sugar with polenta, egg, buttermilk, milk, corn and chillies in bowl; mix until just combined.

2 Spread mixture into prepared pan, sprinkle with extra polenta. Bake in moderate oven about 45 minutes.

SERVES 6

Recipe best made on day of serving

Storage Airtight container
Freeze Suitable
Microwave Not suitable

Diabetic Suitable
Per serve fat 3.7g; 1520kJ

tortilla beef burgers

PREPARATION TIME 45 MINUTES (PLUS CHILLING TIME) • COOKING TIME 35 MINUTES

**1 medium (200g) red
capsicum**

**1 medium (200g) green
capsicum**

8 x 20cm flour tortillas

8 lettuce leaves, shredded

**1/3 cup (80ml) low-fat
sour cream**

**1 tablespoon chopped
fresh parsley**

PATTIES

**310g can red kidney beans,
rinsed, drained**

500g very lean minced beef

**1 small (80g) onion,
chopped finely**

**35g packet taco
seasoning mix**

cooking-oil spray

SALSA

**1 small (80g) onion,
chopped**

**4 medium (300g) egg
tomatoes, chopped**

**1 tablespoon chopped
fresh parsley**

**1 tablespoon mild sweet
chilli sauce**

1 Quarter capsicums, remove seeds and membranes. Grill capsicums, skin-side up, until skin blisters and blackens. Peel skin, slice capsicums.

2 Shape tortillas into cones, place on oven tray, place an individual ovenproof mould in centre of each cone to help keep its shape. Heat tortillas, uncovered, in moderate oven about 5 minutes or until crisp. Fill each tortilla with lettuce, capsicums, patties, salsa and 2 teaspoons sour cream, sprinkle with parsley.

Patties Mash half the beans. Combine beef, all the beans, onion and seasoning mix in bowl; mix well. Shape mixture into 8 patties. Place on oven tray coated with cooking-oil spray, cover, refrigerate 1 hour. Bake, uncovered, in moderately hot oven about 25 minutes or until firm.

Salsa Combine all ingredients in bowl; mix well.

MAKES 8

*Patties and salsa can be made a
day ahead*

Storage Covered, in refrigerator
Freeze Patties suitable
Microwave Not suitable

Diabetic Suitable
Per serve fat 10.1g; 1275kJ

vegetable cheese puffs

PREPARATION TIME 30 MINUTES • COOKING TIME 40 MINUTES

cooking-oil spray

2 teaspoons vegetable oil

60g pumpkin, chopped finely

1 small (100g) red
onion, chopped

1/2 small (40g) carrot, grated

1/4 small (40g) red
capsicum, chopped

1/2 small (50g) zucchini,
grated

15g butter or margarine

1 tablespoon plain flour

1/3 cup (80ml) low-fat milk

1/4 cup (20g) grated
parmesan cheese

2 eggs, separated

1 egg white

1 Coat 4 souffle dishes (3/4 cup/180ml) with cooking-oil spray.

2 Heat oil in non-stick pan, add vegetables, cover, cook until pumpkin is tender. Process vegetables until combined.

3 Melt butter in medium pan, stir in flour, stir over heat until bubbling. Remove from heat, gradually stir in milk, stir over heat until mixture boils and thickens; transfer to large bowl. Stir in vegetable mixture, cheese and egg yolks.

4 Beat all egg whites in small bowl until soft peaks form, fold into vegetable mixture in 2 batches. Spoon mixture into prepared dishes, place on oven tray.

5 Bake in hot oven 10 minutes, reduce heat to moderate, bake further 15 minutes or until puffed. Serve immediately.

SERVES 4

Recipe must be made just before serving

Freeze Not suitable
Microwave Not suitable

Diabetic Additional carbohydrate required
Per serve fat 10.3g; 540kJ

polenta with quick spinach sauté

PREPARATION TIME 30 MINUTES (PLUS CHILLING TIME) • COOKING TIME 35 MINUTES

1 litre (4 cups) chicken stock

1¹/₂ cups (255g) polenta

**1/2 cup (40g) grated
parmesan cheese**

1/4 cup chopped fresh parsley

2 teaspoons olive oil

1 clove garlic, crushed

**1 bunch (500g) English
spinach**

TOMATO MUSHROOM SAUCE

1/2 cup (125ml) water

**1 medium (150g) onion,
chopped finely**

1 clove garlic, crushed

400g can low-salt tomatoes

**1 tablespoon no-salt
tomato paste**

**250g button mushrooms,
halved**

1 Line 20cm x 30cm lamington pan with baking paper. Bring stock to boil
in pan, gradually add polenta, cook, stirring, about 10 minutes or until
polenta is soft and thick.

2 Stir in cheese and parsley. Spread mixture evenly into prepared pan,
cover; refrigerate 2 hours or until firm.

3 Turn polenta out, cut into 16 triangles. Grill polenta until lightly
browned on both sides. Heat oil in large pan, add garlic and spinach,
cook, stirring, until spinach is just wilted. Serve polenta and spinach
with tomato mushroom sauce.

Tomato mushroom sauce Combine water, onion and garlic in pan,
cook, stirring, until onion is soft and water evaporated. Add undrained
crushed tomatoes, paste and mushrooms, simmer, stirring, 5 minutes or
until thickened.

SERVES 4

Polenta and sauce can be made a day ahead

Storage Covered, separately, in refrigerator
Freeze Suitable
Microwave Sauce suitable

Diabetic Suitable
Per serve fat 5.3g; 1300kJ

felafel rolls with tabbouleh

PREPARATION TIME 1 HOUR 45 MINUTES (PLUS STANDING TIME) • COOKING TIME 40 MINUTES

250g frozen broad beans

310g can chickpeas,
 rinsed, drained

2 cloves garlic, crushed

6 green onions, chopped

1 teaspoon ground cumin

1/2 teaspoon ground coriander

1/4 cup chopped fresh parsley

1/4 cup chopped fresh
 mint leaves

2 tablespoons polenta,
 approximately

cooking-oil spray

1 small (130g) green cucumber

8 cos lettuce leaves

400g packet wholemeal
 Lebanese bread

TABBOULEH

2 tablespoons burghul

2/3 cup chopped fresh parsley

2 green onions, chopped finely

1 medium (130g) tomato,
 chopped

1 teaspoon lemon juice

2 teaspoons olive oil

YOGURT SAUCE

1 cup (250ml) low-fat yogurt

1 clove garlic, crushed

2 teaspoons lemon juice

1 teaspoon low-salt soy sauce

2 teaspoons chopped fresh
 mint leaves

1 Place beans in bowl, cover with boiling water, stand 5 minutes. Drain beans, remove skins; drain on absorbent paper.

2 Process beans, chickpeas, garlic, onions, cumin, coriander and herbs until combined. Shape level tablespoons of mixture into patties, roll in polenta, place on oven tray which has been coated with cooking-oil spray. Coat felafel with cooking-oil spray.

3 Bake, uncovered, in hot oven about 40 minutes or until browned.

4 Using a vegetable peeler, cut cucumber into strips lengthways. Divide lettuce, tabbouleh, cucumber, felafel and yogurt sauce between bread, fold over filling.

Tabbouleh Place burghul in small bowl, cover with boiling water. Stand 10 minutes, drain; blot dry with absorbent paper. Combine burghul with remaining ingredients in bowl; mix well.

Yogurt sauce Combine all ingredients in bowl; mix well.

SERVES 4

Felafel can be made a day ahead

Storage Covered, in refrigerator
Freeze Not suitable
Microwave Not suitable

Diabetic Suitable
Per serve fat 6.9g; 1920kJ

chunky chicken and sugar snap pea stir-fry

PREPARATION TIME 10 MINUTES • COOKING TIME 15 MINUTES

2 teaspoons peanut oil

1 medium (150g) onion, chopped

1 medium (200g) red capsicum, sliced

100g sugar snap peas

500g skinless chicken breast fillets, sliced thinly

2 teaspoons cornflour

2/3 cup (160ml) chicken stock

1 tablespoon low-salt soy sauce

1 Heat half the oil in wok, add onion and capsicum, stir-fry over high heat until onion is just soft. Add peas, stir-fry further 1 minute, remove vegetables from wok.

2 Heat remaining oil in wok, add chicken in batches, stir-fry over high heat until browned. Return chicken and vegetables to wok, add blended cornflour, stock and soy sauce, stir until mixture boils and thickens.

SERVES 4

Recipe best made just before serving

Freeze Not suitable
Microwave Not suitable

Diabetic Suitable for occasional use; additional carbohydrate required
Per serve fat 12.6g; 1110kJ

thai-style chicken patties

PREPARATION TIME 25 MINUTES (PLUS CHILLING TIME) • COOKING TIME 15 MINUTES

**2 cups (300g) chopped
    cooked chicken**
1 small (80g) onion, chopped
**1/2 cup (125ml) mild sweet
    chilli sauce**
1 teaspoon fish sauce
**1 tablespoon low-salt
    peanut butter**
1/4 cup (60ml) low-fat yogurt
**1 tablespoon chopped fresh
    coriander leaves**
**1 1/3 cups (90g) wholemeal
    stale breadcrumbs**
cooking-oil spray

1 Process chicken, onion, 2 tablespoons of the chilli sauce, fish sauce, peanut butter, yogurt, coriander and 1 cup of the breadcrumbs until combined.

2 Shape mixture into 4 patties, toss in remaining breadcrumbs; refrigerate 30 minutes.

3 Coat oven tray with cooking-oil spray, place patties on tray; coat patties with cooking-oil spray.

4 Bake, uncovered, in hot oven about 15 minutes or until browned. Turn patties over halfway through cooking. Serve patties with remaining chilli sauce.

MAKES 4

Patties can be made a day ahead
Storage Covered, in refrigerator
Freeze Suitable
Microwave Not suitable

Diabetic Additional carbohydrate required
Per patty fat 10.4g; 1095kJ

main courses

The myriad of main courses found here combine good taste with little fat – and they're so satisfying! We have given you a delicious choice of seafood, chicken and meat, including barbecues and stir-fries, plus tempting vegetarian dishes. Always be sure to check the labels when you are shopping, and use low-fat and low-salt products throughout, as we did.

chicken and lentil cacciatore

PREPARATION TIME 15 MINUTES • COOKING TIME 45 MINUTES

cooking-oil spray

8 (1.5kg) skinless chicken thigh cutlets

1 medium (150g) onion, chopped finely

1 clove garlic, crushed

2 x 400g cans low-salt tomatoes

300g button mushrooms, sliced

1 tablespoon no-salt tomato paste

1 cup (250ml) chicken stock

1/2 teaspoon dried oregano

1/3 cup (65g) red lentils

1/2 cup (80g) seedless black olives

1 tablespoon drained capers

2 tablespoons chopped fresh parsley

1 Heat large non-stick pan, coat with cooking-oil spray, add chicken, cook, turning occasionally until browned, remove.

2 Add onion and garlic to pan, cook, stirring, until onion is soft. Add undrained crushed tomatoes, mushrooms, paste, stock, oregano and lentils. Return chicken to pan, simmer, covered, about 30 minutes or until chicken is tender. Stir in olives, capers and parsley.

SERVES 6

Recipe can be made a day ahead

Storage Covered, in refrigerator
Freeze Suitable
Microwave Suitable

Diabetic Additional carbohydrate required
Per serve fat 7.8g; 1060kJ

tortellini and smoked salmon salad

PREPARATION TIME 15 MINUTES (PLUS COOLING TIME) • COOKING TIME 10 MINUTES

**500g cheese and
   spinach tortellini**
200g smoked salmon
1 tablespoon drained capers
**1 tablespoon chopped
   fresh dill**

DILL YOGURT DRESSING

¹/₄ cup (60ml) low-fat yogurt
**2 tablespoons chopped
   fresh dill**
1 tablespoon honey
2 teaspoons Dijon mustard
1 clove garlic, crushed
2 teaspoons lemon juice

1 Add tortellini to large pan of boiling water, boil, uncovered, until just tender; drain, cool.

2 Cut salmon into strips lengthways, roll up. Combine tortellini, salmon rolls, capers and dill in large bowl, add dressing; mix gently.

3 Serve tortellini mixture over salad leaves, if desired.

Dill yogurt dressing Combine all ingredients in bowl; mix well.

SERVES 4

Recipe can be made 3 hours ahead

Storage Covered, in refrigerator
Freeze Not suitable
Microwave Tortellini suitable

Diabetic Suitable
Per serve fat 8.6g; 1070kJ

baked crumbed fish with parsley caper dressing

PREPARATION TIME 15 MINUTES • COOKING TIME 20 MINUTES

4 (600g) firm white fish fillets

2 tablespoons plain flour

2 egg whites, beaten lightly

1 tablespoon low-fat milk

1¹/₂ cups (105g) stale breadcrumbs

¹/₄ cup (40g) oat bran

¹/₄ cup (40g) polenta

cooking-oil spray

PARSLEY CAPER DRESSING

1 small (80g) onion, chopped finely

1 tablespoon drained capers, chopped finely

1 cup (250ml) low-fat yogurt

1 teaspoon sugar

1 clove garlic, crushed

1 tablespoon chopped fresh parsley

1 Toss fish in flour, shake away excess flour. Dip fish into combined egg whites and milk, then combined breadcrumbs, oat bran and polenta. Place on oven tray which has been coated with cooking-oil spray.

2 Bake in moderately hot oven about 20 minutes or until tender. Serve with parsley caper dressing.

Parsley caper dressing Combine all ingredients in bowl; mix well.

SERVES 4

Recipe can be prepared a day ahead

Storage Covered, separately, in refrigerator
Freeze Uncooked crumbed fish suitable
Microwave Not suitable

Diabetic Additional carbohydrate required
Per serve fat 9.1g; 1765kJ

tamarind fish and vegetables

PREPARATION TIME 10 MINUTES • COOKING TIME 15 MINUTES

2 teaspoons peanut oil

4 (600g) white fish cutlets

150g oyster mushrooms

**1 small (100g) red
  onion, sliced**

2 sticks celery, sliced

200g green beans, halved

1 teaspoon sesame oil

2 teaspoons cornflour

1 cup (250ml) fish stock

1 tablespoon tamarind sauce

2 tablespoons teriyaki sauce

2 teaspoons fish sauce

1 Heat peanut oil in non-stick pan, add fish, cook on both sides until browned and tender, remove from pan; keep warm.

2 Heat same pan, add vegetables, cook, stirring, until vegetables are just tender. Add sesame oil, blended cornflour, stock and sauces to pan, cook, stirring, until mixture boils and thickens slightly.

3 Serve fish with vegetable mixture.

SERVES 4

Recipe best made just before serving

Freeze Not suitable

Microwave Not suitable

Diabetic Additional carbohydrate required

Per serve fat 8g; 865kJ

baked salmon patties with capsicum mayonnaise

PREPARATION TIME 35 MINUTES • COOKING TIME 20 MINUTES

You will need to cook about 2 medium (400g) potatoes for this recipe.

415g can salmon, drained

1 cup mashed potato

2 tablespoons low-fat milk

1 small (80g) onion, grated

¹/₂ teaspoon grated lime rind

**1 tablespoon chopped
  fresh chives**

1 teaspoon chopped fresh dill

1 egg white

**¹/₄ cup (40g) polenta,
  approximately**

cooking-oil spray

CAPSICUM MAYONNAISE

1 medium (200g) red capsicum

**¹/₂ cup (125ml) no-oil herb
  and garlic dressing**

1 teaspoon sugar

¹/₄ cup (60ml) low-fat yogurt

1 teaspoon chopped fresh dill

1 Combine salmon, potato, milk, onion, rind, herbs and egg white
   in bowl; mix well.

2 Shape mixture into 8 patties, coat with polenta, place on oven
   tray coated with cooking-oil spray; refrigerate 30 minutes.

3 Coat patties with cooking-oil spray. Bake, uncovered, in hot oven about
   15 minutes or until browned and hot, turn over halfway through
   cooking. Serve with capsicum mayonnaise.

Capsicum mayonnaise Quarter capsicum, remove seeds and membranes.
Grill capsicum, skin-side up, until skin blisters and blackens. Peel skin,
chop capsicum. Blend or process capsicum, dressing and sugar until
smooth. Add yogurt, process until combined. Stir in dill.

SERVES 4

Patties and mayonnaise can be made a day ahead

Storage Covered, separately, in refrigerator
Freeze Not suitable
Microwave Not suitable

Diabetic Suitable
Per serve fat 9.2g; 1155kJ

prawn and basil risotto

PREPARATION TIME 15 MINUTES • COOKING TIME 45 MINUTES

You will need to cook about 1/2 cup (100g) brown rice for this recipe.

500g medium uncooked prawns

1 stick celery, chopped finely

1 small (100g) onion,
chopped finely

1 cup (250ml) water

1 cup (200g) arborio rice

3 cups (750ml) chicken stock

1 cup (250ml) dry white wine

1 cup cooked brown rice

2 medium (260g) tomatoes,
peeled, seeded, chopped finely

2 tablespoons finely chopped
fresh basil leaves

2 tablespoons finely chopped
fresh parsley

1 Shell and devein prawns, leaving tails intact. Combine celery, onion and water in large pan, cook, stirring occasionally, about 10 minutes or until water has evaporated.

2 Add arborio rice, cook, stirring, 1 minute. Combine stock and wine in separate pan, bring to boil, keep hot. Stir 2/3 cup (160ml) hot stock mixture into rice mixture, cook, stirring, over low heat until liquid is absorbed. Continue adding stock mixture in 1-cup batches, stirring until absorbed before each addition. Total cooking time should be about 35 minutes.

3 Add prawns and brown rice after last addition of stock mixture, cook, stirring, until prawns are just tender. Stir in tomatoes and herbs.

SERVES 4

Recipe best made just before serving

Freeze Not suitable
Microwave Suitable

Diabetic Suitable
Per serve fat 3.1g; 1070kJ

ocean trout with baby vegetables

PREPARATION TIME 25 MINUTES (PLUS COOLING TIME) • COOKING TIME 50 MINUTES

8 baby (200g) beetroot

20 baby (400g) carrots

2 small (180g) zucchini, sliced

**8 baby (320g) new
    potatoes, halved**

4 baby (100g) onions

800g side of ocean trout

TARRAGON LEMON SAUCE

20g butter or margarine

1 clove garlic, crushed

1 small (80g) onion, chopped

1 tablespoon plain flour

3/4 cup (180ml) low-fat milk

**1 tablespoon chopped
    fresh tarragon leaves**

1 teaspoon grated lemon rind

1 tablespoon lemon juice

1 Boil, steam or microwave unpeeled beetroot until just tender, drain. Cool 5 minutes; peel beetroot. Boil, steam or microwave remaining vegetables separately until tender.

2 Remove bones from fish, cut fish diagonally into 4 even pieces. Cut 4 squares (30cm) of baking paper, place a piece of fish on each square. Bring paper around fish to form parcels, seal by folding edges over securely. Place parcels on oven tray.

3 Bake in very slow oven about 20 minutes or until fish is tender. Remove fish from parcels; peel away skin.

4 Serve fish with vegetables and tarragon lemon sauce.

Tarragon lemon sauce Heat butter in pan, add garlic and onion, cook, stirring, until onion is soft. Add flour, cook, stirring, until bubbling. Remove from heat, gradually stir in milk. Stir over heat until mixture boils and thickens. Stir in tarragon, rind and juice.

SERVES 4

Recipe best made just before serving

Freeze Not suitable
Microwave Vegetables suitable

Diabetic Additional carbohydrate required
Per serve fat 11.1g; 1440kJ

spicy prawns

PREPARATION TIME 20 MINUTES (PLUS MARINATING TIME) • COOKING TIME 15 MINUTES

1kg medium uncooked prawns

2 teaspoons peanut oil

MARINADE

2 cloves garlic, crushed

**2 teaspoons grated
  fresh ginger**

**2 teaspoons finely chopped
  lemon grass**

1/2 teaspoon ground cumin

1/2 teaspoon ground coriander

1 tablespoon teriyaki sauce

2 teaspoons honey

4 green onions, chopped

1/2 teaspoon sambal oelek

1 Shell and devein prawns, leaving tails intact. Combine prawns and marinade in bowl. Cover, refrigerate several hours or overnight.

2 Heat oil in large non-stick pan, add prawns in batches, cook prawns until tender.

Marinade Combine all ingredients in bowl; mix well.

SERVES 6

Prawns best cooked just before serving

Freeze Marinated prawns suitable
Microwave Not suitable

Diabetic Additional carbohydrate required
Per serve fat 3g; 615kJ

chilli octopus with fettuccine

PREPARATION TIME 20 MINUTES (PLUS MARINATING TIME) • COOKING TIME 20 MINUTES

1kg baby octopus

2 tablespoons mango chutney

1/3 cup (80ml) lemon juice

**1/4 cup (60ml) no-oil
  French dressing**

2 cloves garlic, crushed

2 tablespoons honey

**2 tablespoons chopped
  fresh coriander leaves**

4 green onions, chopped

500g fettuccine pasta

2 teaspoons vegetable oil

**2 tablespoons chopped
  fresh parsley**

1 Remove and discard heads and beaks from octopus. Combine octopus, chutney, juice, dressing, garlic, honey, coriander and onions in bowl; mix well. Cover, refrigerate several hours or overnight.

2 Drain octopus; reserve marinade. Add pasta to large pan of boiling water, boil, uncovered, until just tender; drain.

3 Heat oil in wok or pan, add octopus in batches; cook over high heat 3 minutes or until tender. Return octopus to pan, add reserved marinade, pasta and parsley, stir until marinade boils.

SERVES 6

Recipe best made close to serving

Freeze Not suitable
Microwave Not suitable

Diabetic Not suitable
Per serve fat 4.6g; 1940kJ

spicy prawns *(front)*
chilli octopus with fettuccine *(back)*

fish parcels with lemon ginger dressing

PREPARATION TIME 30 MINUTES (PLUS STANDING TIME) • COOKING TIME 25 MINUTES

¹/₄ cup (40g) burghul

400g medium uncooked prawns

1 small (150g) red capsicum, chopped finely

2 tablespoons chopped fresh chives

cooking-oil spray

4 (600g) ocean perch fillets

LEMON GINGER DRESSING

2 tablespoons lemon juice

1 teaspoon grated fresh ginger

2 teaspoons chopped fresh dill

¹/₄ teaspoon Sichuan pepper

1 Place burghul in heatproof bowl, cover with boiling water, stand 15 minutes; drain, rinse under cold water, pat dry with absorbent paper. Shell and devein 8 prawns, leaving tails intact. Shell, devein and chop remaining prawns.

2 Combine burghul, chopped prawns, capsicum and chives in medium bowl; mix well.

3 Cut 4 squares (30cm) of baking paper or foil, coat squares with cooking-oil spray. Place a fillet on each square, top with burghul mixture and whole prawns, drizzle with dressing. Fold paper over top, seal ends completely, place parcels on oven tray.

4 Bake in moderate oven 15 minutes, open parcels, bake further 10 minutes or until fish is tender.

Lemon ginger dressing Combine all ingredients in bowl; mix well.

SERVES 4

Recipe can be prepared 2 hours ahead

Storage Covered, in refrigerator
Freeze Not suitable
Microwave Not suitable

Diabetic Additional carbohydrate required
Per serve fat 6.5g; 1145kJ

mushroom, chicken and asparagus risotto

PREPARATION TIME 20 MINUTES • COOKING TIME 1 HOUR

2 medium (320g) skinless
   chicken breast fillets
1 stick celery, chopped
1 green onion, chopped
1/2 small (35g) carrot, chopped
1/2 teaspoon black peppercorns
1 bunch (250g) asparagus
2 teaspoons olive oil
1 clove garlic, crushed
1 large (200g) onion, chopped
250g button mushrooms, sliced
100g shiitake mushrooms,
   sliced finely
2 1/2 cups (500g) quick-cook
   brown rice
1 litre (4 cups) chicken stock
2 cups (500ml) water,
   approximately
100g enoki mushrooms
1 tablespoon chopped
   fresh parsley

1 Combine chicken, celery, onion,
   carrot and peppercorns in pan,
   add enough water to cover
   chicken, simmer, uncovered,
   about 15 minutes or until
   chicken is tender.

2 Remove chicken, strain cooking
   liquid; reserve liquid. Cut
   chicken into thin strips.

3 Boil, steam or microwave
   asparagus until just tender,
   cut into 4cm pieces.

4 Heat oil in large heavy-base
   pan, add garlic, onion, button
   and shiitake mushrooms, cook,
   stirring, until onion is soft;
   stir in rice.

5 Combine reserved liquid, stock
   and enough water to total
   2 litres (8 cups) of liquid in
   another pan, bring to boil,
   keep hot.

6 Stir 2/3 cup (160ml) hot stock
   mixture into rice mixture, cook,
   stirring, over low heat until
   liquid is absorbed. Continue
   adding stock mixture in 1-cup
   batches, stirring, until absorbed
   between each addition. Total
   cooking time should be about
   50 minutes or until rice is tender.

7 Stir in chicken, asparagus, enoki
   mushrooms and parsley, stir
   until hot.

SERVES 6

*Recipe best made just before
serving*

Freeze Not suitable
Microwave Asparagus and chicken
suitable

Diabetic Suitable
Per serve fat 4.9g; 1590kJ

honey sage chicken with fruity seasoning

PREPARATION TIME 30 MINUTES • COOKING TIME 2 HOURS

1.6kg chicken
1 tablespoon low-salt soy sauce
1 tablespoon honey

FRUITY SEASONING

1/2 cup (100g) brown rice
1/4 cup (45g) wild rice
1/4 cup (40g) sultanas
1/4 cup (35g) chopped
**   dried apricots**
1/4 cup chopped fresh chives
1 tablespoon chopped fresh
**   sage leaves**
1 clove garlic, crushed
1 egg white, beaten lightly

SAGE SAUCE

1 teaspoon cornflour
1/4 cup (60ml) dry white wine
3/4 cup (180ml) chicken stock
2 teaspoons chopped fresh
**   sage leaves**
2 teaspoons Worcestershire sauce

1 Remove skin and fat from chicken. Fill chicken with fruity seasoning, secure opening with skewers. Tie legs together, tuck wings under, place chicken on wire rack in baking dish, brush evenly with some of the combined sauce and honey.

2 Bake, uncovered, in moderate oven about 1 1/2 hours or until chicken s tender, brushing during first half of cooking with honey mixture. Cover legs and wings with foil during cooking if chicken is browning too quickly.

3 Serve chicken with sage sauce.

Fruity seasoning Add brown rice to large pan of boiling water, stir to separate grains, boil, uncovered, 25 minutes or until just tender; drain. Add wild rice to large pan of boiling water, stir to separate grains, boil, uncovered, 20 minutes or until just tender; drain. Combine rices with remaining ingredients; mix well.

Sage sauce Combine blended cornflour and wine with remaining ingredients in pan, stir until sauce boils and thickens.

SERVES 6

Seasoning can be made a day ahead

Storage Covered, in refrigerator
Freeze Not suitable
Microwave Sage sauce suitable

Diabetic Suitable; additional carbohydrate required if seasoning is not eaten
Per serve fat 7.6g; 1440kJ

curried vegetable and lentil flan

PREPARATION TIME 40 MINUTES (PLUS CHILLING) • COOKING TIME 1 HOUR 15 MINUTES (PLUS COOLING TIME)

cooking-oil spray

1/2 cup (100g) red lentils

1 cup (160g) wholemeal
plain flour

1/4 cup (35g) white plain flour

60g low-fat cream cheese

1 egg white, beaten lightly

2 teaspoons low-fat milk,
approximately

2 eggs, beaten lightly

1 egg white, extra

1/4 cup (60ml) low-fat
milk, extra

1/3 cup (40g) grated low-fat
cheddar cheese

FILLING

2 teaspoons vegetable oil

1 medium (120g)
zucchini, grated

1 medium (120g)
carrot, grated

1 medium (125g)
parsnip, grated

1 small (200g) leek, sliced

1 clove garlic, crushed

1/4 teaspoon sambal oelek

3 teaspoons mild curry powder

2 teaspoons caraway seeds

1 tablespoon chopped
fresh coriander leaves

1 Coat 24cm round loose-base
flan tin with cooking-oil spray.

2 Add lentils to pan of boiling
water, boil, uncovered, about
8 minutes or until just tender;
drain, cool.

3 Sift flours into bowl, rub in
cream cheese. Add 1/2 cup of the
lentils (reserve remaining lentils
for filling), egg white and
enough milk to make ingredients
cling together. Press dough into
a ball, knead gently on floured
surface until smooth. Cover,
refrigerate 30 minutes.

4 Roll pastry between sheets of
baking paper until large enough
to line prepared tin. Lift pastry
into tin, ease into side, trim
edge. Lightly prick base with
fork, refrigerate 30 minutes.
Cover pastry with baking paper,
fill with dried beans or rice, place
on oven tray. Bake in moderately
hot oven 15 minutes. Remove
paper and beans carefully from
pastry case, bake further
15 minutes or until browned; cool.

5 Spoon filling into prepared case.

Pour over combined eggs, extra
egg white and extra milk,
sprinkle with cheddar cheese.
Bake in moderately hot oven
about 30 minutes or until set.

Filling Heat oil in pan, add
vegetables, garlic and sambal
oelek, cook, stirring, until
vegetables are soft. Stir in curry
powder and seeds, cook, stirring,
until fragrant. Stir in reserved
lentils and coriander.

SERVES 6

Recipe can be made a day ahead

Storage Covered, in refrigerator
Freeze Uncooked pastry suitable
Microwave Lentils suitable

Diabetic Suitable
Per serve fat 7.9g; 960kJ

lentil patties with spicy eggplant sauce

PREPARATION TIME 50 MINUTES (PLUS CHILLING) • COOKING TIME 1 HOUR 25 MINUTES (PLUS COOLING)

**2 medium (400g) old
    potatoes, chopped**
2/3 cup (130g) red lentils
1 medium (200g) red capsicum
cooking-oil spray
**1 medium (150g) onion,
    chopped finely**
2 cloves garlic, crushed
2 tablespoons water
1 stick celery, chopped finely
**2 (160g) silverbeet leaves,
    chopped finely**
**1/4 cup (40g) pine nuts,
    toasted, chopped**
**1 1/2 cups (105g) stale
    breadcrumbs**
**2 teaspoons chopped
    fresh coriander leaves**
**1 tablespoon chopped
    fresh parsley**
**1/2 cup (50g) packaged
    breadcrumbs, approximately**
2 teaspoons vegetable oil

SPICY EGGPLANT SAUCE

1 large (500g) eggplant
1 clove garlic, crushed
2 tablespoons lemon juice
**1 tablespoon chopped
    fresh parsley**
**1 tablespoon mild sweet
    chilli sauce**
1/4 cup (60ml) low-fat yogurt

1 Boil, steam or microwave
   potatoes until tender. Drain
   potatoes, mash well. Add lentils
   to pan of boiling water, boil,
   uncovered, about 8 minutes
   or until tender; drain.

2 Quarter capsicum, remove and
   discard seeds and membranes.
   Grill capsicum, skin-side up,
   until skin blisters and blackens.
   Peel away skin, chop capsicum.

3 Coat non-stick pan with
   cooking-oil spray, add onion and
   garlic, cook, stirring, 1 minute.
   Add water and celery, cook,
   stirring, until water has nearly
   evaporated. Add silverbeet,
   cook, stirring, until wilted.

4 Combine mashed potato, lentils,
   capsicum, onion mixture, pine
   nuts, stale breadcrumbs and
   herbs in bowl; mix well. Shape
   mixture into 6 patties. Toss
   patties in packaged
   breadcrumbs, press crumbs on
   firmly, cover, refrigerate 1 hour.

5 Heat oil in non-stick pan, cook
   patties until browned on both
   sides. Serve with spicy
   eggplant sauce.

Spicy eggplant sauce Cut
eggplant in half lengthways,
place cut-side down on oven
tray coated with cooking-oil
spray. Coat eggplant with
cooking oil spray. Bake,
uncovered, in moderate oven
about 45 minutes or until
eggplant is soft; cool. Scoop out
flesh, discard skin. Blend or
process eggplant with remaining
ingredients until combined.

SERVES 6

Recipe can be made a day ahead

Storage Covered, in refrigerator
Freeze Not suitable
Microwave Potatoes suitable

Diabetic Suitable
Per serve fat 7.9g; 1075kJ

gingered pork with stir-fried vegetables

PREPARATION TIME 15 MINUTES (PLUS MARINATING TIME) • COOKING TIME 40 MINUTES

1/4 cup (60ml) low-salt
  soy sauce
2 tablespoons dry red wine
1 tablespoon golden syrup
1 tablespoon brown sugar or
  powdered artificial sweetener
2 cloves garlic, crushed
1 tablespoon grated
  fresh ginger
2 (500g) lean pork fillets
2 teaspoons peanut oil
1 medium (150g) onion,
  chopped coarsely
1 small (70g) carrot,
  sliced finely
1 medium (120g)
  zucchini, sliced
2 teaspoons cornflour
150g snow peas, halved
1 1/4 cups (100g) bean sprouts

1 Combine sauce, wine, golden syrup, sugar, garlic and ginger in bowl, add pork; mix well. Cover, refrigerate several hours or overnight, turning occasionally.

2 Drain pork, reserve marinade. Add pork to heated non-stick pan, cook until browned all over. Transfer pork to wire rack in baking dish.

3 Bake, uncovered, in moderate oven about 30 minutes or until tender. Slice diagonally.

4 Heat oil in wok or pan, add onion, carrot and zucchini, stir-fry over high heat until tender.

5 Blend cornflour with reserved marinade and enough water to make 1 cup (250ml) liquid. Add to wok with snow peas and sprouts, stir until sauce boils and thickens slightly.

6 Serve pork with stir-fried vegetables.

SERVES 4

Recipe best made just before serving

Freeze Not suitable
Microwave Not suitable

Diabetic Additional carbohydrate required
Per serve fat 3.3g; 830kJ

spicy chinese pork spare ribs

PREPARATION TIME 10 MINUTES (PLUS MARINATING TIME) • COOKING TIME 40 MINUTES

**2kg lean American-style
  pork spare ribs**
1 tablespoon honey
2 tablespoons sweet sherry
1 tablespoon teriyaki sauce
1/2 teaspoon five spice powder
2 cloves garlic, crushed
**2 teaspoons grated
  fresh ginger**
1 teaspoon sesame oil
**1/4 cup (60ml) low-salt
  soy sauce**
1 teaspoon sambal oelek
**2 tablespoons chopped
  fresh coriander leaves**
1 teaspoon Sichuan pepper

1 Cut ribs into serving pieces (about 3 bones per serving). Combine ribs with remaining ingredients in bowl, cover, refrigerate several hours or overnight.

2 Drain ribs, reserve marinade. Place ribs in single layer on wire racks in baking dishes.

3 Bake in moderately hot oven about 40 minutes or until tender. Brush with reserved marinade during cooking.

SERVES 4

Recipe can be prepared 2 days ahead

Storage Covered, in refrigerator
Freeze Suitable
Microwave Not suitable

Diabetic Additional carbohydrate required
Per serve fat 4.3g; 1035kJ

roast pork with rosemary

PREPARATION TIME 20 MINUTES • COOKING TIME 50 MINUTES (PLUS COOLING TIME)

1 teaspoon olive oil
2 cloves garlic, crushed
1 tablespoon chopped
   fresh rosemary
1 large (200g) onion, chopped
150g button mushrooms, sliced
1 bunch (500g) English
   spinach, chopped roughly
3 x 200g lean pork fillets

SAUCE

1 teaspoon cornflour
1/2 cup (125ml) chicken stock
1/2 teaspoon balsamic vinegar
1/2 teaspoon chopped
   fresh rosemary

1 Heat oil in non-stick pan, add garlic, rosemary, onion and mushrooms, cook, stirring, until onion is soft. Add spinach, cook, stirring, until spinach is just wilted; cool.

2 Cut a pocket in each fillet, fill with spinach mixture. Tie fillets at 1.5cm intervals. Add pork to pan, cook until browned all over. Place pork on wire rack in baking dish.

3 Bake in moderately hot oven about 40 minutes or until cooked through; reserve juices for sauce. Serve pork with sauce.

Sauce Combine blended cornflour, reserved pan juices and stock, vinegar and rosemary in small pan, stir until the sauce boils and thickens slightly.

SERVES 4

Filling can be prepared several hours ahead

Storage Covered, in refrigerator
Freeze Not suitable
Microwave Filling suitable

Diabetic Additional carbohydrate required
Per serve fat 4g; 810kJ

pork with pear and apple sauce

PREPARATION TIME 10 MINUTES (PLUS MARINATING TIME) • COOKING TIME 20 MINUTES

4 (600g) lean pork
   butterfly steaks
2 tablespoons low-salt
   soy sauce
1 tablespoon lemon juice
1 tablespoon honey
1 clove garlic, crushed
3 teaspoons chopped
   fresh thyme

PEAR AND APPLE SAUCE

10g butter or margarine
1 medium (180g) pear,
   quartered
1 large (200g) apple,
   quartered
8 small (80g) spring
   onions, halved

2 teaspoons sugar
1 teaspoon cornflour
1/2 cup (125ml) chicken stock
1/4 cup (60ml) water

1 Combine pork with remaining ingredients in bowl, cover, refrigerate several hours or overnight.

2 Drain pork, reserve marinade. Heat non-stick pan, add pork, cook until browned on both sides and tender.

3 Serve pork with pear and apple sauce.

Pear and apple sauce Heat butter in pan, add fruit, onions and sugar, cook, stirring about

5 minutes or until fruit is lightly browned. Add 1/4 cup (60ml) reserved marinade, blended cornflour, stock and water, bring to boil, simmer, covered, stirring occasionally, about 5 minutes or until fruit is tender.

SERVES 4

Sauce can be made a day ahead

Storage Covered, in refrigerator
Freeze Not suitable
Microwave Not suitable

Diabetic Additional carbohydrate required
Per serve fat 3.5g; 855kJ

Roast pork with rosemary *(top)*
Pork with pear and apple sauce *(right)*

baked potatoes mornay

PREPARATION TIME 20 MINUTES • COOKING TIME 1 HOUR 20 MINUTES (PLUS COOLING TIME)

4 large (1.2kg) potatoes

FILLING

1/2 bunch (125g) asparagus, chopped

20g butter or margarine

1 tablespoon plain flour

3/4 cup (180ml) low-fat milk

1/3 cup (40g) grated low-fat cheddar cheese

3 green onions, chopped finely

105g can salmon, drained

1 Pierce potato skins in several places with a skewer or fork. Place potatoes on oven tray.

2 Bake in moderately hot oven about 1 hour or until tender; cool 10 minutes.

3 Cut tops from potatoes, scoop out half the flesh with a spoon, leaving skins intact. Combine chopped potato with filling, divide mixture between potato shells.

4 Bake potatoes, uncovered, in moderately hot oven about 15 minutes.

Filling Boil, steam or microwave asparagus until just tender; drain. Heat butter in pan, stir in flour, stir over heat until mixture is bubbly. Remove from heat, gradually stir in milk, stir over heat until mixture boils and thickens. Remove from heat, stir in cheese, onions, salmon and asparagus.

SERVES 4

Filling can be made a day ahead

Storage Covered, in refrigerator
Freeze Not suitable
Microwave Suitable

Diabetic Suitable
Per serve fat 8.3g; 1415kJ

lamb and spinach soup with risoni

PREPARATION TIME 20 MINUTES • COOKING TIME 40 MINUTES

1/2 cup (110g) risoni pasta

1 large (350g) red capsicum

cooking-oil spray

350g lean lamb fillets,
   sliced thinly

1/2 cup (125ml) water

1 small (200g) leek, sliced

2 cloves garlic, crushed

1 teaspoon chopped
   fresh rosemary

1 tablespoon no-salt
   tomato paste

11/2 cups (375ml)
   vegetable stock

1.5 litres (6 cups) water, extra

1 chicken stock cube

1 small (90g) zucchini,
   halved, sliced

4 (320g) silverbeet
   leaves, shredded

1 Add risoni to pan of boiling water, boil, uncovered, until just
   tender; drain.

2 Quarter capsicum, remove seeds and membranes. Grill capsicum,
   skin-side up, until skin blisters and blackens. Peel skin, cut capsicum
   into 1cm strips.

3 Coat large non-stick pan with cooking-oil spray, add lamb in batches,
   cook until browned all over, remove from pan.

4 Add water, leek, garlic and rosemary to pan, cook, stirring, until almost
   all the water has evaporated. Add paste, stock, extra water and crumbled
   stock cube; boil, uncovered, 10 minutes. Reduce heat then simmer,
   covered, 10 minutes.

5 Return lamb to pan, add zucchini; simmer, covered, until zucchini
   is tender. Add silverbeet, risoni and capsicum, stir until hot.

SERVES 6

Recipe can be made a day ahead

Storage Covered, in refrigerator
Freeze Not suitable
Microwave Risoni suitable

Diabetic Additional carbohydrate required
Per serve fat 3g; 615kJ

spicy grilled chicken

PREPARATION TIME 10 MINUTES (PLUS MARINATING TIME) • COOKING TIME 10 MINUTES

**4 single (640g) skinless
  chicken breast fillets**
1/4 cup (60ml) lemon juice
1/4 cup (60ml) dry white wine
1 tablespoon honey
**2 tablespoons chopped
  fresh coriander leaves**
**1 tablespoon grated
  fresh ginger**
**2 small fresh red
  chillies, chopped**
2 cloves garlic, crushed
2 teaspoons ground turmeric
2 teaspoons cumin seeds
1/2 teaspoon ground cinnamon
2 strips lemon rind
cooking-oil spray

1 Cut 3 slashes in each fillet. Blend or process juice, wine, honey, coriander, ginger, chillies, garlic, turmeric, seeds and cinnamon until smooth. Cut rind into thin strips, combine rind, chicken and pureed mixture in bowl, cover, refrigerate several hours or overnight.

2 Drain chicken, reserve marinade. Heat barbecue or heavy griddle pan, coat with cooking-oil spray, add chicken, cook on both sides until tender, brushing with reserved marinade during cooking.

SERVES 4

Chicken can be prepared a day ahead

Storage Covered, in refrigerator
Freeze Uncooked marinated chicken suitable
Microwave Not suitable

Diabetic Additional carbohydrate required
Per serve fat 4.4g; 820kJ

barbecued chicken and lentil salad

PREPARATION TIME 30 MINUTES (PLUS MARINATING TIME) • COOKING TIME 30 MINUTES

1/2 cup (125ml) low-fat yogurt

1 teaspoon cracked
   black pepper

1 clove garlic, crushed

1 tablespoon chopped fresh
   basil leaves

1/2 teaspoon ground turmeric

1 tablespoon hoisin sauce

4 single (640g) skinless
   chicken breast fillets

cooking-oil spray

1 radicchio lettuce

LENTIL SALAD

1 medium (200g) red capsicum

1 medium (200g) yellow
   capsicum

1 cup (200g) brown lentils

1 litre (4 cups) water

1 clove garlic, flattened

1/3 cup (80ml) red wine vinegar

1/2 teaspoon sugar

2 teaspoons olive oil

1 bunch (350g) baby
   curly endive

1 Combine yogurt, pepper, garlic, basil, turmeric and sauce in bowl, add chicken, mix well. Cover, refrigerate 1 hour.

2 Remove chicken from marinade; discard marinade. Heat barbecue or griddle pan, coat with cooking-oil spray, add chicken, cook on both sides until browned and tender.

3 Slice chicken thinly, combine with lentil salad. Place radicchio on serving plate, top with salad mixture.

Lentil salad Quarter capsicums, remove seeds and membranes, grill capsicums, skin-side up, until skin blisters and blackens. Peel skin, finely chop capsicums.

Combine lentils, water and garlic in pan, bring to boil, simmer, uncovered, about 15 minutes or until lentils are just tender; drain, discard garlic. Combine lentils and capsicums in bowl, mix well.

Combine vinegar, sugar and half the oil in jar; shake well. Pour vinegar mixture over lentil mixture; mix well. Heat large pan, add half the remaining oil and half the endive, cook, stirring, until just wilted. Repeat with remaining oil and endive. Combine endive with lentil mixture.

SERVES 4

Lentil salad can be made a day ahead without endive

Storage Covered, in refrigerator
Freeze Not suitable
Microwave Endive suitable
Diabetic Suitable
Per serve fat 11.1g; 1635kJ

chicken and wild rice paella

PREPARATION TIME 25 MINUTES • COOKING TIME 45 MINUTES

**8 (300g) medium
uncooked prawns**
8 small mussels
1/3 cup (60g) wild rice
**4 (560g) skinless chicken
thigh cutlets**
1 small (200g) leek, chopped
2 cloves garlic, crushed
**1 medium (200g) yellow
capsicum, chopped**
**1 medium (200g) red
capsicum, chopped**
1 teaspoon sambal oelek
**2 tablespoons chopped
fresh thyme**
1 cup (200g) basmati rice
1/4 cup (60ml) dry white wine
1/2 teaspoon saffron threads
2 cups (500ml) chicken stock
2 tablespoons drained capers
**2 medium (240g) yellow
zucchini, chopped**
1 cup fresh parsley

1 Shell and devein prawns,
discarding heads and leaving
tails intact. Scrub mussels,
remove beards.

2 Add wild rice to pan of boiling
water, boil, uncovered, about
20 minutes or until tender,
drain, rinse, drain well.

3 Heat large pan, add chicken,
cook on both sides until
browned but not cooked
through. Remove from pan;
drain on absorbent paper.
Remove bones from chicken,
slice chicken.

4 Drain all but 1 tablespoon of
drippings from pan, add leek,
garlic, capsicums, sambal oelek
and thyme, cook, stirring,
5 minutes. Add basmati rice,
wine, saffron, stock and chicken,
cook, covered, about 12 minutes
or until rice is just tender. Add
seafood, capers, zucchini and
wild rice, cook, covered, further
5 minutes or until seafood
is tender.

5 Serve sprinkled with parsley.

SERVES 6

Recipe best made close to serving
Freeze Not suitable
Microwave Not suitable

Diabetic Suitable
Per serve fat 6.1g; 1415kJ

warm minted lamb salad

PREPARATION TIME 30 MINUTES (PLUS MARINATING TIME) • COOKING TIME 15 MINUTES (PLUS STANDING)

400g lean lamb fillets

1 clove garlic, crushed

2 tablespoons lemon juice

1/3 cup (80ml) chicken stock

1/2 cup (100g) couscous

cooking-oil spray

**3 medium (390g) tomatoes,
    peeled, seeded**

1 small (130g) green cucumber

150g mixed salad leaves

**2 tablespoons chopped
    fresh mint leaves**

DRESSING

3/4 cup (80ml) low-fat yogurt

3 teaspoons lemon juice

1/4 cup (60ml) water

pinch ground cumin

1 clove garlic, crushed

1 teaspoon low-salt soy sauce

1 Combine lamb, garlic and juice in bowl; mix well, cover, refrigerate several hours or overnight.

2 Bring stock to boil in pan, add couscous, remove from heat, stir, cover, stand 5 minutes or until stock is absorbed.

3 Heat pan, coat with cooking-oil spray, add couscous, cook, stirring, until grains are separated. Remove from pan, cool.

4 Slice tomatoes thinly. Slice cucumber thinly with vegetable peeler.

5 Heat barbecue or griddle pan, coat with cooking oil spray, add lamb, cook, turning, until cooked as desired. Cut lamb into thin slices. Place salad leaves, cucumber, tomatoes and lamb on serving plate. Drizzle with dressing, sprinkle with mint and couscous.

Dressing Combine all ingredients in small bowl; mix well.

SERVES 4

Recipe can be prepared a day ahead

Storage Covered, separately, in refrigerator
Freeze Not suitable
Microwave Not suitable

Diabetic Additional carbohydrate required
Per serve fat 4.7g; 885kJ

italian pork steaks with baked capsicum salad

PREPARATION TIME 20 MINUTES • COOKING TIME 1 HOUR 10 MINUTES

4 (600g) lean pork
   butterfly steaks

1/2 teaspoon cracked
   black pepper

1/2 teaspoon dried
   oregano leaves

cooking-oil spray

1 teaspoon cornflour

1 cup (250ml) chicken stock

2 teaspoons red wine vinegar

BAKED CAPSICUM SALAD

2 medium (400g)
   yellow capsicums

cooking-oil spray

2 large (180g) egg
   tomatoes, halved

90g button mushrooms, sliced

4 cloves garlic, crushed

1/4 teaspoon dried
   oregano leaves

2 teaspoons olive oil

16 (80g) seedless black olives

2 tablespoons grated
   parmesan cheese

1 Sprinkle pork with pepper and oregano. Heat large pan, coat with cooking-oil spray, add pork, cook until tender; remove. Add blended cornflour and stock to pan, stir until mixture boils and thickens, add vinegar. Return pork to pan, stir until hot.

2 Serve with baked capsicum salad.

Baked capsicum salad Cut capsicums in half, remove seeds and membranes, place capsicums on oven tray coated with cooking-oil spray. Fill capsicums with tomatoes, mushrooms and garlic. Sprinkle with oregano and oil. Bake, uncovered, in moderately hot oven 40 minutes. Add olives, sprinkle with cheese, bake further 15 minutes or until capsicums are tender.

SERVES 4

Recipe can be made a day ahead

Storage Covered, in refrigerator
Freeze Not suitable
Microwave Not suitable

Diabetic Additional carbohydrate required
Per serve fat 8.7g; 1035kJ

grilled chicken in lime chilli marinade

PREPARATION TIME 10 MINUTES (PLUS MARINATING TIME) • COOKING TIME 10 MINUTES

4 single (640g) skinless chicken breast fillets

cooking-oil spray

2 tablespoons chopped fresh coriander leaves

1 lime

LIME CHILLI MARINADE

1/3 cup (80ml) lime juice

1 clove garlic, crushed

2 teaspoons grated fresh ginger

1 tablespoon low-salt soy sauce

1 small fresh red chilli, chopped finely

2 spring onions, chopped

1 Pound chicken fillets with a mallet to an even thickness. Combine chicken and marinade in bowl, cover, refrigerate several hours or overnight.

2 Drain chicken; discard marinade. Heat barbecue or grill pan, coat with cooking-oil spray, add chicken, cook on both sides until browned and tender.

3 Sprinkle with coriander, serve with lime wedges.

Lime chilli marinade Combine all ingredients in bowl; mix well.

SERVES 4

Recipe can be prepared a day ahead

Storage Covered, in refrigerator
Freeze Suitable
Microwave Not suitable

Diabetic Additional carbohydrate required
Per serve fat 4.4g; 780kJ

crunchy spiced chicken

PREPARATION TIME 20 MINUTES (PLUS CHILLING TIME) • COOKING TIME 40 MINUTES

4 (1.2kg) chicken marylands
1/4 cup (35g) plain flour
2 cups (140g) wholemeal
  stale breadcrumbs
1/3 cup (35g) Corn
  Flake Crumbs
1 teaspoon ground coriander
2 teaspoons ground cumin
2 teaspoons garlic salt
3 egg whites, beaten lightly
cooking-oil spray

1 Cut each maryland through joint into leg and thigh pieces; remove skin. Place chicken in large pan of cold water, bring to boil; drain. Pat dry with absorbent paper.

2 Toss chicken in flour, shake away excess flour. Combine crumbs, spices and salt; mix well. Dip chicken in egg whites, then crumb mixture. Place chicken on oven tray which has been coated with cooking-oil spray, cover, refrigerate 1 hour.

3 Coat chicken lightly with cooking-oil spray, bake, uncovered, in moderately hot oven about 30 minutes or until tender.

SERVES 4

Recipe can be prepared a day ahead

Storage Covered, in refrigerator
Freeze Not suitable
Microwave Not suitable

Diabetic Additional carbohydrate required
Per serve fat 10.4g; 1590kJ

herb-crusted lamb with braised vegetables

PREPARATION TIME 20 MINUTES • COOKING TIME 1 HOUR 10 MINUTES

¹/₄ cup (50g) pearl barley

¹/₃ cup chopped
**   fresh parsley**

2 tablespoons chopped
**   fresh coriander leaves**

1 tablespoon chopped
**   fresh thyme**

1 tablespoon Cajun
**   seasoning**

4 (800g) trim lamb
**   eyes of loin**

1 teaspoon vegetable oil

1 medium (170g) red
**   onion, sliced**

1 small (425g) fennel
**   bulb, sliced**

2 medium (250g) parsnips,
**   chopped coarsely**

1 bunch (20) baby carrots

1 medium (200g) red
**   capsicum, chopped**

¹/₂ cup (125ml) beef stock

¹/₄ cup (60ml) dry
**   white wine**

1 tablespoon balsamic
**   vinegar**

1 bunch (300g) baby bok
**   choy, chopped roughly**

1 Add barley to large pan of boiling water, boil, uncovered, about 30 minutes or until tender, drain.

2 Combine herbs and seasoning in bowl, coat lamb with herb mixture. Place lamb on baking-paper-covered oven tray.

3 Bake, uncovered, in moderately hot oven about 15 minutes or until lamb is cooked as desired; keep warm.

4 Heat oil in non-stick pan, add onion and fennel, cook, stirring, until onion is soft. Add parsnips, carrots, capsicum, stock, wine and vinegar, simmer, covered, about 15 minutes or until vegetables are tender. Add barley and bok choy, cook, stirring, until bok choy is just wilted.

5 Serve lamb sliced with braised vegetables.

SERVES 4

Barley can be cooked a day ahead

Storage Covered, in refrigerator
Freeze Not suitable
Microwave Barley and vegetables suitable

Diabetic Additional carbohydrate required
Per serve fat 8.4g; 1375kJ

warm pasta and lamb salad

PREPARATION TIME 15 MINUTES (PLUS MARINATING TIME) • COOKING TIME 35 MINUTES

500g lean lamb fillets, sliced

2 teaspoons olive oil

3 teaspoons sugar

1/3 cup (80ml) lemon juice

1 tablespoon dry red wine

**1 tablespoon mild sweet
  chilli sauce**

1 clove garlic, crushed

**2 tablespoons chopped
  fresh rosemary**

**4 medium (300g) egg
  tomatoes, quartered**

500g spiral pasta

cooking-oil spray

1/2 cup (125ml) beef stock

**2 tablespoons chopped
  fresh parsley**

**1 bunch (500g) English
  spinach, chopped roughly**

1 Combine lamb, oil, 1 teaspoon of the sugar, juice, wine, sauce, garlic and rosemary in bowl, cover, refrigerate 3 hours or overnight.

2 Drain lamb, reserve marinade. Place tomatoes in single layer on oven tray, sprinkle with remaining sugar.

3 Bake, uncovered, in moderate oven 20 minutes.

4 Meanwhile add pasta to large pan of boiling water, boil, uncovered, until just tender; drain.

5 Coat non-stick pan with cooking-oil spray, add lamb in batches, cook until browned and tender. Return lamb to pan, add reserved marinade, stock and parsley, stir until mixture boils.

6 Gently toss with pasta, tomatoes and spinach.

SERVES 6

Recipe best made close to serving

Freeze Not suitable
Microwave Pasta suitable

Diabetic Suitable
Per serve fat 6.6g; 1840kJ

veal pizzaiola

PREPARATION TIME 10 MINUTES • COOKING TIME 20 MINUTES

4 (500g) lean veal steaks

1¹/₂ tablespoons plain flour

2 teaspoons olive oil

1 clove garlic, crushed

2 tablespoons dry white wine

**1 tablespoon chopped
fresh oregano**

¹/₂ cup (125ml) beef stock

**3 cups (750ml) bottled
pasta sauce**

**1 tablespoon chopped
fresh parsley**

**²/₃ cup (100g) seedless
black olives**

1 Toss veal in flour, shake away excess flour. Heat oil in large pan, add veal, cook over high heat until browned on both sides and tender; remove from pan.

2 Add garlic, then wine and oregano, simmer until reduced by half. Add stock and sauce, simmer, uncovered, about 10 minutes or until sauce thickens slightly.

3 Return veal to pan, add parsley and olives, stir until hot.

SERVES 4

Recipe best made just before serving

Freeze Not suitable
Microwave Not suitable

Diabetic Additional carbohydrate required
Per serve fat 7.1g; 1250kJ

lentil, vegetable and brown rice pilaf

PREPARATION TIME 10 MINUTES • COOKING TIME 40 MINUTES

1 stick celery, chopped

1 medium (120g)
   carrot, chopped

1 medium (150g)
   onion, chopped

1 teaspoon ground cumin

2 teaspoons mild curry powder

1 teaspoon celery salt

1 cup (200g) brown lentils

1/2 cup (100g) brown rice

1 litre (4 cups) water

1 teaspoon grated fresh ginger

2 tablespoons chopped
   fresh parsley

1 Combine celery, carrot, onion, cumin, curry powder, salt, lentils, rice, water and ginger in medium pan, bring to boil, simmer, covered, about 40 minutes or until rice is tender and water absorbed.

2 Serve sprinkled with parsley.

SERVES 4

Recipe best made just before serving

Freeze Not suitable
Microwave Suitable

Diabetic Suitable
Per serve fat 1.6g; 930kJ

steak with honey, thyme and mustard glaze

PREPARATION TIME 5 MINUTES • COOKING TIME 15 MINUTES

2 teaspoons olive oil

4 lean (600g) New York-style beef steaks

2 tablespoons honey

¹/₃ cup (80ml) lemon juice

2 teaspoons chopped fresh thyme

1 tablespoon seeded mustard

1 clove garlic, crushed

1 Heat oil in pan, add steaks, cook until done as desired; remove from pan. Add remaining ingredients to pan, simmer, uncovered, until mixture thickens slightly.

2 Serve glaze over steaks.

SERVES 4

Recipe best made just before serving

Freeze Not suitable

Microwave Not suitable

Diabetic Not suitable

Per serve fat 8.1g; 980kJ

chicken, kumara and pasta stir-fry

PREPARATION TIME 30 MINUTES • COOKING TIME 25 MINUTES

**500g skinless chicken breast
fillets, sliced**
**1/3 cup shredded fresh
basil leaves**
**1/4 cup (60ml) white
wine vinegar**
2 tablespoons lemon juice
1 teaspoon sugar
3 cloves garlic, crushed
1 1/2 tablespoons olive oil
300g coloured fettuccine
**1 small (250g) kumara,
sliced**
1 large (200g) onion, sliced
150g snow peas, sliced

1　Combine chicken, 1/4 cup of
basil, vinegar, juice, sugar,
garlic and half the oil in bowl,
cover, refrigerate several hours
or overnight.

2　Drain chicken; reserve marinade.
Add pasta to large pan of
boiling water, boil, uncovered,
until just tender; drain.

3　Meanwhile, boil, steam or
microwave kumara until almost
tender; drain.

4　Heat remaining oil in wok or
pan. Add onion, stir-fry over
high heat until soft, remove.
Add chicken in batches, stir-fry
until browned.

5　Add kumara, cook, stirring,
3 minutes. Return onion to pan
or wok with reserved marinade,
pasta and snow peas, cook,
stirring, until marinade boils.
Sprinkle with remaining basil.

SERVES 6

*Recipe best made just before
serving*

Freeze Not suitable
Microwave Kumara suitable

Diabetic Suitable
Per serve fat 8g; 1270kJ

accompaniments

With the fresh, fabulous flavour combinations of these recipes, we've created the variety you need to keep you interested in healthy eating. They're easy, versatile and add colour and appeal to any main meal. Always be sure to check the labels when you are shopping, and use low-fat and low-salt products throughout, as we did.

caramelised parsnips, carrots and sage

PREPARATION TIME 15 MINUTES • COOKING TIME 45 MINUTES

4 large (720g) parsnips
4 medium (480g) carrots
1/4 cup (60ml) honey
1 tablespoon water
1 tablespoon olive oil
2 tablespoons chopped fresh sage leaves
2 tablespoons brown sugar
1 tablespoon chopped fresh parsley

1 Peel parsnips and carrots, cut in half, then into quarters lengthways. Combine honey, water and oil in large bowl, whisk until combined, add vegetables; mix well.

2 Pour vegetable mixture into baking dish, sprinkle with sage. Bake, uncovered, in moderately hot oven about 40 minutes or until vegetables are tender. Sprinkle vegetables with sugar, grill until lightly browned. Serve sprinkled with parsley.

SERVES 4

Recipe best made close to serving

Freeze Not suitable
Microwave Not suitable

Diabetic Not suitable
Per serve fat 5.5g; 1045kJ

radicchio capsicum salad

PREPARATION TIME 20 MINUTES
• COOKING TIME 30 MINUTES

3 large (270g) egg tomatoes

2 teaspoons sugar

1 medium (200g) yellow capsicum

1 medium (200g) red capsicum

1 medium (120g) carrot

**1 medium bunch (300g)
   curly endive**

1 large radicchio lettuce

DRESSING

1 tablespoon olive oil

**1/4 cup (60ml) red
   wine vinegar**

1 clove garlic, crushed

**2 teaspoons mild sweet
   chilli sauce**

**1 tablespoon chopped
   fresh parsley**

1 Quarter tomatoes. Place tomatoes, cut-side up,
   on oven tray, sprinkle with sugar, bake, uncovered,
   in moderate oven about 30 minutes.

2 Quarter capsicums, remove seeds and membranes.
   Grill capsicums, skin-side up, until skin blisters
   and blackens. Peel skin, slice capsicums.

3 Peel carrot into thin strips, roll up strips. Combine
   tomatoes, capsicums, carrot, endive and torn
   radicchio leaves in large bowl, drizzle with dressing;
   mix well.

   Dressing Combine all ingredients in jar; shake well.

SERVES 6

Recipe best made close to serving

Freeze Not suitable
Microwave Not suitable

Diabetic Suitable
Per serve fat 3.4g; 150kJ

brussels sprouts with garlic and honey

PREPARATION TIME 15 MINUTES
• COOKING TIME 15 MINUTES

750g brussels sprouts

20 baby (400g) carrots

cooking-oil spray

1 medium (150g) onion, sliced

**1/4 cup (60ml) white
   wine vinegar**

2 teaspoons olive oil

2 cloves garlic, crushed

1 tablespoon honey

**2 teaspoons chopped
   fresh parsley**

1 Trim outer leaves and bases of sprouts. Make a cut
   about 3mm deep across each base. Boil, steam or
   microwave sprouts and carrots separately until just
   tender; drain, rinse under cold water, drain.

2 Coat non-stick pan with cooking-oil spray, add
   onion, cook, stirring, until soft. Add sprouts and
   carrots, cook, stirring, 3 minutes. Add combined
   vinegar, oil, garlic, honey and parsley, cook,
   stirring, until liquid is reduced by half.

SERVES 4

Recipe best made close to serving

Freeze Not suitable
Microwave Sprouts and carrots suitable

Diabetic Suitable
Per serve fat 3.8g; 380kJ

radiccho capsicum salad *(top)*
lime and chilli broccoli *(centre)*
brussels sprouts with garlic and honey *(right)*

lime and chilli broccoli

PREPARATION TIME 10 MINUTES
• COOKING TIME 5 MINUTES

1kg broccoli, chopped
1/3 cup (80ml) mild sweet chilli sauce
2 tablespoons low-salt soy sauce
2 teaspoons grated lime rind
2 teaspoons lime juice
1 tablespoon chopped fresh coriander leaves

1 Boil, steam or microwave broccoli until just tender; drain.

2 Serve topped with combined remaining ingredients.

SERVES 6

Recipe best made just before serving

Freeze Not suitable
Microwave Broccoli suitable

Diabetic Suitable
Per serve fat 0.5g; 165kJ

cheese-topped kumara casserole

PREPARATION TIME 20 MINUTES • COOKING TIME 35 MINUTES

cooking-oil spray

2 large (1kg) kumara

**1 medium (170g) red
  onion, sliced**

1 clove garlic, crushed

1/2 cup (125ml) chicken stock

40g butter or margarine

1/4 cup (35g) plain flour

1 1/4 cups (310ml) low-fat milk

**1/4 cup (60ml) chicken
  stock, extra**

**1 teaspoon chopped
  fresh thyme**

**1/2 cup (35g) wholemeal
  breadcrumbs**

**1/4 cup (30g) grated low-fat
  cheddar cheese**

1 Coat ovenproof dish (1.5 litre/6 cup) with cooking-oil spray. Cut kumara into 5mm slices.

2 Combine kumara, onion, garlic and stock in pan, cover, simmer until kumara is tender; drain.

3 Place kumara mixture in prepared dish. Melt butter in pan, stir in flour, stir over heat until bubbling. Remove from heat, gradually stir in combined milk and extra stock, stir over heat until sauce boils and thickens, stir in thyme.

4 Pour sauce over kumara, top with combined breadcrumbs and cheese. Bake in moderately hot oven about 20 minutes or until browned.

SERVES 6

Recipe best made on day of serving

Freeze Not suitable
Microwave Kumara suitable

Diabetic Suitable
Per serve fat 7.1g; 980kJ

asparagus and oregano barley risotto

PREPARATION TIME 15 MINUTES • COOKING TIME 1 HOUR 25 MINUTES

1/4 cup (50g) pearl barley

1 large (350g) red capsicum

**3 bunches (750g)
  asparagus, chopped**

1 teaspoon olive oil

1 small (200g) leek, chopped

1 clove garlic, crushed

1/4 cup chopped fresh oregano

2 cups (400g) arborio rice

2 cups (500ml) water

1/2 cup (125ml) dry white wine

1 litre (4 cups) chicken stock

1/2 teaspoon ground nutmeg

**1/3 cup (25g) grated
  parmesan cheese**

**1 teaspoon freshly
  ground pepper**

1 Add barley to large pan of boiling water, boil, uncovered, about
   30 minutes or until tender; drain.

2 Quarter capsicum, remove seeds and membranes. Grill capsicum,
   skin-side up, until skin blisters and blackens. Peel skin, slice capsicum.
   Boil, steam or microwave asparagus until just tender; drain, rinse under
   cold water, drain well.

3 Heat oil in pan, add leek and garlic, cook, stirring, until leek is soft.
   Add oregano and rice, stir until combined.

4 Combine water, wine and stock in separate pan, bring to boil, keep hot.
   Stir 1/2 cup (125ml) hot stock mixture into rice mixture, cook, stirring,
   over low heat until liquid is absorbed. Continue adding stock mixture,
   in 1-cup batches, stirring, until absorbed between each addition. Total
   cooking time should be about 35 minutes or until rice is just tender.

5 Stir in barley, red capsicum, asparagus and remaining ingredients;
   stir until hot.

SERVES 6

Recipe best made close to serving

Freeze Not suitable

Microwave Suitable

Diabetic Suitable

Per serve fat 2.8g; 1360kJ

creamy vegetable risotto timbales

PREPARATION TIME 20 MINUTES • COOKING TIME 1 HOUR (PLUS COOLING TIME)

cooking-oil spray

1 medium (150g) onion, chopped finely

1 medium (120g) carrot, chopped finely

1/2 cup (125ml) water

1 clove garlic, crushed

1 cup (200g) arborio rice

3 cups (750ml) chicken or vegetable stock

1 tablespoon chopped fresh chives

1 tablespoon chopped fresh basil leaves

1/2 cup (40g) grated parmesan cheese

1 egg, beaten lightly

1 Coat four moulds (1 cup/250ml) with cooking-oil spray, cover bases with baking paper. Combine onion, carrot, water and garlic in pan, cook, stirring, until water has evaporated. Add rice, cook, stirring, 1 minute.

2 Bring stock to boil in another pan, keep hot. Stir $2/3$ cup (160ml) of hot stock into rice mixture, cook, stirring, over low heat until liquid is absorbed.

3 Continue adding stock in 1-cup batches, stirring, until absorbed between each addition. Total cooking time should be about 35 minutes or until rice is just tender. Stir in herbs and cheese. Cool 10 minutes.

4 Stir egg into mixture. Divide mixture evenly between prepared moulds, place on oven tray.

5 Bake, uncovered, in hot oven about 25 minutes or until firm.

SERVES 4

Recipe can be made a day ahead

Storage Covered, in refrigerator
Freeze Not suitable
Microwave Suitable

Diabetic Suitable
Per serve fat 5g; 1020kJ

green beans with tomatoes and oregano

PREPARATION TIME 10 MINUTES • COOKING TIME 10 MINUTES

600g green beans
1 tablespoon olive oil
1 small (100g) red onion,
  chopped finely
6 medium (450g) egg
  tomatoes, sliced thickly
1 teaspoon sugar
1 tablespoon balsamic vinegar
1 tablespoon water
1 tablespoon chopped
  fresh oregano

1 Add beans to pan of boiling water, boil 2 minutes; drain, rinse under cold water, drain.

2 Heat oil in pan, add onion, cook, stirring, until soft. Add tomatoes and sugar, cook, stirring, 2 minutes or until tomatoes are just soft. Stir in vinegar, water and oregano.

3 Place beans on serving plate, top with tomato mixture. Serve warm or cold.

SERVES 6

Recipe can be made 3 hours ahead

Storage Covered, in refrigerator
Freeze Not suitable
Microwave Suitable

Diabetic Suitable
Per serve fat 3.6g; 270kJ

cabbage, zucchini and capsicum stir-fry

PREPARATION TIME 15 MINUTES • COOKING TIME 10 MINUTES

375g thin egg noodles
1 tablespoon peanut oil
1 medium (170g) red
  onion, sliced
2 medium (240g)
  zucchini, sliced
1 large (350g) red
  capsicum, sliced
1/2 medium (300g) Chinese
  cabbage, chopped
1/2 teaspoon dried
  crushed chillies
1 teaspoon fish sauce
1 tablespoon low-salt
  soy sauce
1/2 cup (125ml)
  vegetable stock
2 tablespoons brown
  malt vinegar
1/2 teaspoon brown sugar
1 cup (80g) bean sprouts
1/3 cup chopped fresh
  coriander leaves

1 Add noodles to large pan of boiling water, boil, uncovered, until just tender; drain.

2 Heat oil in wok or pan, add onion, zucchini, capsicum and cabbage, cook, stirring, until onion is soft.

3 Add chillies, sauces, stock, vinegar and sugar, cook, stirring, until mixture boils, remove from heat, stir in sprouts and coriander; mix well.

4 Serve with noodles.

SERVES 4

Recipe best made just before serving

Freeze Not suitable
Microwave Not suitable

Diabetic Suitable
Per serve fat 5.6g; 705kJ

new potato salad with mustard dill dressing

PREPARATION TIME 10 MINUTES • COOKING TIME 10 MINUTES

24 baby (1kg) new potatoes
1/3 cup (80ml) low-fat
  sour cream
1/3 cup (80ml) low-fat yogurt
1 teaspoon chopped fresh dill
1 tablespoon seeded mustard
2 tablespoons no-oil herb and
  garlic dressing

1 Boil, steam or microwave potatoes until just tender; drain, cool.

2 Combine potatoes with combined remaining ingredients in bowl; toss gently.

SERVES 6

Recipe can be prepared several hours ahead

Storage Covered in refrigerator
Freeze Not suitable
Microwave Potatoes suitable

Diabetic Suitable
Per serve fat 2.8g; 610kJ

warm bean and pasta salad

PREPARATION TIME 10 MINUTES • COOKING TIME 30 MINUTES

400g penne
150g green beans, sliced
2 medium (240g) zucchini,
  sliced
1 small (80g) onion,
  chopped finely
1/2 cup (125ml) water
1 clove garlic, crushed
2 x 400g cans low-salt
  tomatoes
2 tablespoons no-salt
  tomato paste
1 teaspoon chicken
  stock powder
50g fetta cheese, crumbled
2 tablespoons grated
  parmesan cheese
2 tablespoons chopped
  fresh parsley

1 Add pasta to large pan of boiling water, boil, uncovered, until just tender; drain.

2 Add beans and zucchini to separate pans of boiling water, boil 2 minutes; drain, rinse under cold water, drain.

3 Combine onion, water and garlic in pan, cook, stirring, until water has evaporated. Stir in undrained crushed tomatoes, paste and stock powder, simmer, uncovered, about 15 minutes or until thickened slightly.

4 Combine pasta, beans, zucchini and tomato sauce in large bowl; serve sprinkled with cheeses and parsley.

SERVES 6

Tomato sauce can be made a day ahead

Storage Covered, in refrigerator
Freeze Not suitable
Microwave Suitable

Diabetic Suitable
Per serve fat 5.3g; 1350kJ

warm bean and pasta salad *(top)*
new potato salad with mustard dill dressing *(right)*

bok choy and spinach stir-fried salad

PREPARATION TIME 10 MINUTES • COOKING TIME 15 MINUTES

1 teaspoon peanut oil

1 teaspoon sesame oil

**1 small (130g) green
    cucumber, sliced**

1 medium (120g) carrot, sliced

**1/2 bunch (250g) English
    spinach, chopped**

**1 bunch (500g) baby bok
    choy, chopped**

1 tablespoon oyster sauce

**1 tablespoon low-salt
    soy sauce**

2 tablespoons rice wine

**1 tablespoon brown
    malt vinegar**

2 tablespoons chopped fresh coriander leaves

4 green onions, chopped

1 tablespoon cornflour

1 cup (250ml) vegetable stock

1 Heat oils in wok or pan, add cucumber and carrot, stir-fry over high heat until carrot is almost tender.

2 Add spinach and bok choy, stir-fry until just wilted. Add sauces, wine, vinegar, coriander, onions and blended cornflour and stock, stir until mixture boils and thickens slightly.

SERVES 4

Recipe best made just before serving

Freeze Not suitable
Microwave Not suitable

Diabetic Suitable
Per serve fat 3.1g; 290kJ

jacket potatoes with herbed cottage cheese

PREPARATION TIME 15 MINUTES • COOKING TIME 1 HOUR

6 large (1.8kg) old potatoes

cooking-oil spray

250g low-fat cottage cheese

3 green onions, chopped finely

2 tablespoons grated parmesan cheese

2 tablespoons chopped fresh basil leaves

1 tablespoon chopped fresh chives

1 Pierce skin of potatoes in several places with fork or skewer. Place potatoes on oven tray which has been coated with cooking-oil spray

2 Bake in moderately hot oven about 1 hour or until tender. Cut a 5cm-deep cross in each potato, gently press sides to open cross. Serve topped with combined remaining ingredients.

SERVES 6

Cottage cheese mixture can be made a day ahead

Storage Covered, in refrigerator
Freeze Not suitable
Microwave Potatoes suitable

Diabetic Suitable
Per serve fat 3g; 1110kJ

crunchy herb roasted potatoes

PREPARATION TIME 10 MINUTES • COOKING TIME 1 HOUR

4 medium (800g) potatoes
cooking-oil spray
1/2 teaspoon fine sea salt
1/2 teaspoon seasoned pepper
12 small fresh rosemary sprigs

1 Cut each potato into thin slices, three-quarters of the way through. Place potatoes on baking-paper-lined oven tray, coat potatoes with cooking-oil spray. Sprinkle with salt and pepper, top with rosemary sprigs.

2 Bake in moderately hot oven about 1 hour or until crisp and tender.

SERVES 4

Recipe best made close to serving

Freeze Not suitable
Microwave Not suitable

Diabetic Suitable
Per serve fat 0.9g; 555kJ

baked herb polenta with onions and cheese

PREPARATION TIME 15 MINUTES • COOKING TIME 25 MINUTES (PLUS COOLING AND CHILLING TIME)

1 cup (250ml) low-fat milk
1 1/2 cups (375ml)
   vegetable stock
1 1/2 cups (375ml) water
1 1/2 cups (250g) polenta
1/2 cup (60g) grated low-fat
   cheddar cheese
1 teaspoon chopped
   fresh parsley
1 teaspoon chopped
   fresh oregano
1 teaspoon chopped
   fresh thyme
cooking-oil spray
20g butter or margarine
1/4 cup (60ml) water, extra
8 spring onions, chopped
2/3 cup (80g) grated low-fat
   cheddar cheese, extra

1 Grease 20cm x 30cm lamington pan, cover base and sides with baking paper.

2 Bring milk, stock and water to boil in pan, gradually add polenta, cook, stirring, about 10 minutes or until polenta is soft and thick; cool 1 minute. Stir in cheese and herbs.

3 Spread mixture evenly into prepared pan, cover, refrigerate 2 hours or until firm.

4 Turn polenta out, cut into 8 pieces. Place polenta on oven tray which has been coated with cooking-oil spray. Combine butter and extra water in pan, add onions, cook, stirring, until onions are soft and water has evaporated. Top polenta with onion mixture and extra cheese.

5 Bake in moderate oven about 15 minutes or until cheese is melted.

SERVES 8

Polenta can be made 2 days ahead

Storage Covered, in refrigerator
Freeze Not suitable
Microwave Not suitable

Diabetic Suitable
Per serve fat 6.9g; 810kJ

crunchy herb roasted potatoes *(top)*
baked herb polenta with onions and cheese *(right)*

red capsicum and coriander couscous

PREPARATION TIME 10 MINUTES • COOKING TIME 20 MINUTES (PLUS STANDING TIME)

**2 cups (500ml)
vegetable stock**

20g butter or margarine

2 cups (400g) couscous

2 large (700g) red capsicums

cooking-oil spray

1 small (200g) leek, sliced

2 tablespoons water

**2 tablespoons chopped fresh
coriander leaves**

**2 tablespoons pine
nuts, toasted**

**1/4 cup (60ml) balsamic
vinegar**

1 Bring stock to boil in pan, add butter and couscous, remove from heat, stir, cover, stand 5 minutes or until stock is absorbed; cool.

2 Quarter capsicums, remove seeds and membranes. Grill capsicums, skin-side up, until skin blisters and blackens. Peel skin, slice capsicums.

3 Coat non-stick pan with cooking-oil spray, add leek and water, cook, stirring, over low heat until leek is soft. Combine couscous, capsicum, leek, coriander, nuts and vinegar in large bowl; mix well.

SERVES 6

Recipe can be made 3 hours ahead

Storage Covered, in refrigerator
Freeze Not suitable
Microwave Leek suitable

Diabetic Suitable
Per serve fat 8.8g; 1195kJ

caramelised chokoes and baby onions

PREPARATION TIME 15 MINUTES • COOKING TIME 15 MINUTES

4 medium (1.4kg) chokoes
10g butter or margarine
¼ cup (50g) brown sugar
¼ cup (60ml) chicken stock
6 baby (150g) onions, halved
2 tablespoons balsamic vinegar
1 tablespoon chopped
  fresh parsley

1 Peel chokoes, cut each into 8 wedges. Heat butter in pan, add chokoes, sugar and stock, simmer, covered, 5 minutes, stirring occasionally. Stir in onions and vinegar, cook, covered, about 5 minutes or until chokoes and onions are tender, stirring occasionally.

2 Simmer few more minutes or until chokoes and onions are lightly browned. Serve sprinkled with parsley.

SERVES 6

Recipe best made close to serving

Freeze Not suitable
Microwave Suitable

Diabetic Not suitable
Per serve fat 1.8g; 360kJ

roasted eggplants with tomato and fetta

PREPARATION TIME 20 MINUTES (PLUS STANDING TIME) • COOKING TIME 1 HOUR 10 MINUTES

2 small (460g) eggplants
coarse cooking salt
2 medium (260g) tomatoes
2 tablespoons white
** wine vinegar**
1 clove garlic, crushed
1 teaspoon olive oil
1 teaspoon sugar
30g fetta cheese
1 tablespoon shredded
** fresh basil leaves**

1 Cut eggplants in half lengthways. Keeping stems intact, cut each half lengthways into 4 slices. Place slices on wire rack over tray, sprinkle with salt, stand 30 minutes. Rinse slices well, pat dry with absorbent paper.

2 Cut tomatoes into 5mm slices. Place a tomato slice between eggplant slices, place on baking-paper-covered oven tray. Drizzle with combined vinegar, garlic, oil and sugar, top with crumbled cheese.

3 Bake, covered, in moderately hot oven 35 minutes. Brush vegetables with pan juices, bake, uncovered, further 35 minutes or until browned. Serve sprinkled with basil.

SERVES 4

Recipe can be prepared 3 hours ahead

Storage Covered, in refrigerator
Freeze Not suitable
Microwave Not suitable

Diabetic Suitable
Per serve fat 2.9g; 235kJ

caraway cabbage with crispy ham

PREPARATION TIME 10 MINUTES • COOKING TIME 15 MINUTES

cooking-oil spray

6 slices (130g) lean ham,
sliced thinly

2 small (160g) onions, sliced

3/4 cup (180ml) chicken stock

1 small (1.2kg) cabbage,
shredded coarsely

1 teaspoon caraway seeds

2 tablespoons chopped
fresh parsley

1 Coat large non-stick pan with cooking-oil spray, add ham, cook, stirring, over high heat until ham is crisp; remove from pan. Add onions and 1/2 cup (125ml) of the stock to pan, cook, stirring, about 5 minutes or until onions are soft.

2 Add cabbage, remaining stock and seeds, cook, covered, about 5 minutes or until cabbage is tender. Stir in parsley and about quarter of the ham. Serve topped with remaining ham.

SERVES 6

Recipe best made close to serving

Freeze Not suitable
Microwave Not suitable

Diabetic Suitable
Per serve fat 1.5g; 290kJ

corn and chilli kidney beans

PREPARATION TIME 15 MINUTES

310g can red kidney beans, rinsed, drained

250g cherry tomatoes, halved

1 small (100g) red onion, sliced

310g can corn kernels, rinsed, drained

2 tablespoons chopped fresh coriander leaves

1 small fresh red chilli, seeded, chopped

2 tablespoons lime juice

$1/2$ teaspoon sugar

1 Combine all ingredients in bowl; mix well.

SERVES 4

Recipe best made just before serving

Freeze Not suitable

Diabetic Suitable

Per serve fat 1.2g; 590kJ

garlic roasted baby potatoes

PREPARATION TIME 5 MINUTES
● COOKING TIME 45 MINUTES

24 baby (1kg) new potatoes

1 teaspoon olive oil

1 teaspoon Sichuan pepper

18 unpeeled cloves garlic

6 sprigs fresh thyme

1 Combine all ingredients in baking dish; mix well.

2 Bake, uncovered, in moderately hot oven about 45 minutes or until potatoes are browned and tender, stirring twice during cooking.

SERVES 6

Recipe best made just before serving

Freeze Not suitable

Microwave Not suitable

Diabetic Suitable

Per serve fat 1g; 475kJ

snake beans with almonds

PREPARATION TIME 15 MINUTES
● COOKING TIME 15 MINUTES

2 bunches (820g) snake beans, chopped

1 teaspoon olive oil

1 medium (150g) onion, sliced thinly

1 small fresh red chilli, seeded, chopped

2 tablespoons brown sugar

1/3 cup (80ml) brown malt vinegar

1/2 cup (40g) flaked almonds, toasted

2 teaspoons chopped fresh coriander leaves

1 Boil, steam or microwave beans until tender; drain.
Heat oil in pan, add onion and chilli; cook, stirring,
until onion is soft. Add sugar and vinegar; cook,
stirring, until sugar is dissolved. Stir in nuts and
coriander; cook, stirring, until hot, stir in beans.

SERVES 6

Recipe best made close to serving

Freeze Not suitable
Microwave Suitable

Diabetic Suitable
Per serve fat 5g; 430kJ

mexican-style coleslaw

PREPARATION TIME 20 MINUTES

4 cups (320g) shredded cabbage

1 small (100g) red onion, chopped

1 bunch (350g) radishes, sliced thinly

1 medium (200g) red capsicum, chopped

1/4 cup chopped fresh coriander leaves

DRESSING

2 tablespoons lime juice

2 tablespoons mild sweet chilli sauce

1 clove garlic, crushed

1 Combine all ingredients in bowl, add dressing; mix.

Dressing Combine all ingredients in jar; shake well.

SERVES 4

Recipe can be made several hours ahead

Storage Covered, in refrigerator
Freeze Not suitable

Diabetic Suitable
Per serve fat 0.3g; 105kJ

tabbouleh rice salad

PREPARATION TIME 20 MINUTES (PLUS STANDING TIME)

You will need to cook about 1 cup (200g) brown rice for this recipe.

1/2 cup (80g) burghul

2 cups cooked brown rice

2 tomatoes (350g), chopped

4 green onions, sliced

1/2 cup chopped fresh
   flat-leafed parsley

1/3 cup chopped fresh
   mint leaves

2 tablespoons lemon juice

1 tablespoon olive oil

2 cloves garlic, crushed

1/2 teaspoon sugar

1 Place burghul in heatproof bowl, cover with boiling water; stand 15 minutes. Rinse burghul, drain well, pat dry on absorbent paper.

2 Combine burghul with remaining ingredients in bowl; mix well.

SERVES 6

Recipe can be made several hours ahead

Storage Covered, in refrigerator
Freeze Not suitable
Microwave Rice suitable

Diabetic Suitable
Per serve fat 5.1g; 1275kJ

saucy bok choy, sprouts and noodles

PREPARATION TIME 10 MINUTES • COOKING TIME 10 MINUTES

375g flat rice noodles

1 teaspoon peanut oil

80g snow peas, halved

1 bunch (500g) baby bok choy, sliced

3 cups (240g) bean sprouts

1 tablespoon cornflour

¹/₄ cup (60ml) oyster sauce

³/₄ cup (180ml) vegetable stock

1 Add noodles to pan of boiling water; drain immediately.

2 Heat oil in wok or pan, add snow peas, bok choy and sprouts, cook, stirring, until bok choy is just wilted. Add blended cornflour, sauce and stock, stir until mixture boils and thickens. Serve over noodles.

SERVES 4

Recipe best made just before serving

Freeze Not suitable

Microwave Not suitable

Diabetic Suitable

Per serve fat 2.3g; 1400kJ

desserts

Indulgences within your low-fat eating plan can include the prettiest fruit treats, plus ice-creams, cakes, pancakes, meringues and strudels – even chocolate mousse and a rich trifle! Always be sure to check the labels when you are shopping, and use low-fat and low-salt products throughout, as we did.

poached pears, date and orange compote

PREPARATION TIME 40 MINUTES (PLUS COOLING AND CHILLING TIME) • COOKING TIME 20 MINUTES

4 medium (720g) firm pears
3 medium (540g) oranges
2 cups (500ml) apple juice
1/2 cup (125ml) orange juice
1 cup (250ml) water
1/3 cup (75g) caster sugar or
  powdered artificial
  sweetener
1 cinnamon stick
12 (250g) fresh dates,
  seeded, halved
2 tablespoons Cointreau

SPICED CREAM

1/3 cup (65g) low-fat ricotta
  cheese, sieved
1/2 cup (125ml) low-fat
  sour cream
1 tablespoon honey or
  powdered artificial
  sweetener
1/2 teaspoon ground cinnamon

1 Peel pears. Using a canelle knife, cut grooves into pears at an angle. Using vegetable peeler, peel rind thinly from 1 orange, cut rind into strips. Peel remaining oranges, discard seeds and pith, cut all oranges between membranes into segments.

2 Combine juices, water, sugar and cinnamon in large pan, stir over heat, without boiling, until sugar is dissolved. Add pears and rind, simmer, covered, about 15 minutes or until pears are just tender.

3 Place pears in large heatproof bowl, pour hot syrup over pears. Add orange segments, dates and liqueur; cool. Cover, refrigerate 3 hours or overnight. Serve compote with spiced cream.

Spiced cream Combine all ingredients in bowl; mix well.

SERVES 8

Compote and spiced cream can be made a day ahead

Storage Covered, separately, in refrigerator
Freeze Not suitable
Microwave Not suitable

Diabetic Suitable
Per serve fat 4g; 1205kJ

rhubarb and strawberry mousse sponge cake

PREPARATION TIME 50 MINUTES (PLUS CHILLING TIME) • COOKING TIME 35 MINUTES (PLUS COOLING TIME)

cooking-oil spray

2 eggs

1 egg white

1/3 cup (75g) caster sugar

1 teaspoon vanilla essence

1/3 cup (50g) self-raising flour

1/4 cup (30g) packaged ground almonds

MOUSSE

4 stems (250g) fresh rhubarb, chopped

2 tablespoons caster sugar

2 tablespoons water

250g strawberries

1/2 cup (100g) low-fat ricotta cheese, sieved

100g packaged low-fat cream cheese

3 teaspoons gelatine

2 tablespoons water, extra

2 egg whites

1 tablespoon caster sugar, extra

1 Coat deep 22cm round cake pan with cooking-oil spray, cover base with baking paper. Combine eggs, egg white, sugar and essence in small bowl, beat with electric mixer until thick and creamy.

2 Gently fold in sifted flour and nuts. Pour mixture into prepared pan, bake in moderate oven about 25 minutes or until just firm. Cool on wire rack.

3 Split cold cake into 2 layers. Cover base and side of 20cm springform tin with foil. Place 1 cake layer in prepared tin, pour mousse over cake, top with remaining layer of cake. Cover with plastic wrap, refrigerate several hours or overnight.

4 Remove cake from tin, dust with sifted icing sugar and decorate with extra berries, if desired.

Mousse Combine rhubarb, sugar and water in small pan, simmer, uncovered, until rhubarb is soft, stirring occasionally; cool. Blend or process rhubarb mixture, strawberries, ricotta and cream cheese until smooth; transfer to large bowl. Sprinkle gelatine over extra water in cup, stand in small pan of simmering water, stir until dissolved. Stir into rhubarb mixture.

Beat egg whites in small bowl until soft peaks form, gradually add extra sugar, beat until dissolved. Fold egg white mixture into rhubarb mixture in 2 batches.

SERVES 8

Recipe best made a day ahead

Storage Covered, in refrigerator
Freeze Not suitable
Microwave Gelatine suitable

Diabetic Not suitable
Per serve fat 7.9g; 800kJ

chocolate mousse

PREPARATION TIME 25 MINUTES (PLUS CHILLING TIME) • COOKING TIME 5 MINUTES

1 tablespoon gelatine

2 tablespoons water

**75g reduced-fat milk
    chocolate, melted**

1 tablespoon dry instant coffee

**2 tablespoons drinking
    chocolate**

2 tablespoons Frangelico

**1/2 cup (125ml) low-fat
    sour cream**

1/2 cup (125ml) low-fat yogurt

4 egg whites

**1/4 cup (55g) caster
    sugar or powdered
    artificial sweetener**

1 Sprinkle gelatine over water in cup, stand in small pan of simmering water, stir until dissolved. Combine chocolate, coffee, drinking chocolate and liqueur in large bowl. Stir in combined cream and yogurt, then gelatine mixture.

2 Beat egg whites in small bowl with electric mixer until soft peaks form, gradually add sugar, beating until dissolved between additions. Fold egg white mixture into chocolate mixture in 2 batches.

3 Spoon mixture into 6 dessert glasses (3/4 cup/180ml). Refrigerate until set. Serve with fruit, if desired.

SERVES 6

Recipe can be made a day ahead

Storage Covered, in refrigerator
Freeze Not suitable
Microwave Gelatine and chocolate suitable

Diabetic Suitable
Per serve fat 6.7g; 630kJ

oranges in caramel syrup

PREPARATION TIME 20 MINUTES (PLUS CHILLING TIME) • COOKING TIME 15 MINUTES

4 large (1.2kg) oranges
¼ cup (40g) seedless dates
⅓ cup (75g) caster sugar
½ cup (125ml) water
1 cinnamon stick
1 tablespoon Grand Marnier
¼ cup (60ml) low-fat
  sour cream
1 tablespoon icing
  sugar mixture

1 Peel oranges, discard seeds and pith; cut between membranes into segments. Cut dates into thin strips. Combine orange segments and dates in heatproof bowl.

2 Combine sugar, water and cinnamon in medium heavy-based pan, stir over heat, without boiling, until sugar is dissolved. Bring to boil, simmer, uncovered, without stirring, until mixture is a dark caramel colour.

3 Pour caramel over oranges in bowl; mix well. Stir in liqueur, cover, refrigerate several hours (toffee will dissolve in refrigerator), stirring every hour. Serve with combined cream and icing sugar.

SERVES 4

Recipe can be made a day ahead

Storage Covered, separately, in refrigerator
Freeze Not suitable
Microwave Not suitable

Diabetic Not suitable
Per serve fat 3.3g; 920kJ

vanilla ice-cream with mango and berry coulis

PREPARATION TIME 30 MINUTES (PLUS COOLING AND FREEZING TIME) • COOKING TIME 10 MINUTES

We used boysenberries in this recipe. Fresh or frozen berries are suitable.

1/4 cup (30g) custard powder

3 cups (750ml) low-fat milk

1/2 cup (110g) caster sugar or powdered artificial sweetener

300g soft tofu

2 teaspoons vanilla essence

BERRY COULIS

300g berries

1 tablespoon icing sugar mixture or powdered artificial sweetener

MANGO COULIS

1 medium (430g) mango, chopped

1/3 cup (80ml) water, approximately

1 Blend custard powder with a little of the milk until smooth. Combine blended custard powder with remaining milk and sugar in pan, stir until custard boils and thickens, remove from heat.

2 Blend or process tofu until smooth. Stir tofu and essence into custard; cool.

3 Transfer mixture to 14cm x 21cm loaf pan, cover, freeze until just firm. Transfer mixture to bowl; beat with electric mixer until smooth, return to pan, cover; freeze until firm.

4 Repeat beating and freezing twice. Alternatively, churn ice-cream in an ice-cream machine according to manufacturer's instructions. Serve vanilla ice-cream with mango and berry coulis.

Berry coulis Blend or process berries until smooth. Push mixture through a coarse sieve, combine puree with sifted icing sugar.

Mango coulis Blend or process mango until smooth, add enough water to give pouring consistency.

SERVES 6

Ice-cream and coulis can be made 3 days ahead

Storage Ice-cream, covered, in freezer. Coulis, covered, in refrigerator
Microwave Not suitable

Diabetic Suitable
Per serve fat 4.6g; 1000kJ

starfruit and mango trifle with orange jelly

PREPARATION TIME 40 MINUTES (PLUS CHILLING TIME) • COOKING TIME 40 MINUTES (PLUS CHILLING TIME)

You will need about 3 passionfruit for this recipe.

cooking-oil spray

3 eggs

1/3 cup (75g) caster sugar

1/2 cup (75g) self-raising flour

2 teaspoons ground ginger

10g butter or margarine, melted

1 tablespoon boiling water

1/4 cup (60ml) Grand Marnier or Cointreau

200g blueberries

2 medium (300g) starfruit, sliced thinly

2 small (600g) mangoes, sliced

1/4 cup (60ml) passionfruit pulp

ORANGE JELLY

1 1/2 tablespoons gelatine

1/4 cup (55g) caster sugar

1 cup (250ml) water

2 cups (500ml) orange juice

CUSTARD

1/4 cup (30g) custard powder

1 tablespoon caster sugar

2 1/2 cups (625ml) low-fat milk

1 Coat deep 20cm round cake pan with cooking-oil spray, cover base with baking paper.

2 Beat eggs and sugar in small bowl with electric mixer until thick and creamy. Transfer mixture to large bowl. Gently fold in sifted flour and ginger, then combined butter and water.

3 Spread mixture into prepared pan, bake in moderate oven about 25 minutes. Turn onto wire rack to cool.

4 Cut sponge into 3cm squares, place over base and side of serving bowl (3 litre/12 cup), sprinkle with liqueur, pour in partly set jelly, refrigerate until set. Place half the fruit over jelly, add custard. Decorate with remaining fruit.

Orange jelly Combine gelatine, sugar and water in medium pan, stir over heat, without boiling, until sugar is dissolved. Remove from heat, add juice; refrigerate until jelly is partly set.

Custard Blend custard powder and sugar with a little of the milk in pan, stir in remaining milk. Stir over heat until custard boils and thickens. Remove from heat; cover, cool.

SERVES 8

Recipe can be made a day ahead

Storage Covered, in refrigerator
Freeze Not suitable
Microwave Orange jelly and custard suitable

Diabetic Not suitable
Per serve fat 3.8g; 1120kJ

plum and apple strudel with vanilla yogurt

PREPARATION TIME 45 MINUTES • COOKING TIME 45 MINUTES (PLUS COOLING TIME)

2 large (400g) apples,
    peeled, cored
825g can whole dark
    plums, drained
2 teaspoons grated
    lemon rind
1/3 cup (65g) firmly packed
    brown sugar
1/4 cup (60ml) maple-
    flavoured syrup
1/4 cup (60ml) water
1 cinnamon stick
1/2 cup (60g) packaged
    ground almonds
6 sheets fillo pastry
cooking-oil spray

VANILLA YOGURT

1/3 cup (80ml) low-fat milk
3/4 cup (180ml)
    low-fat yogurt
2 teaspoons vanilla essence
1/4 cup (40g) icing
    sugar mixture

1 Cut each apple into 12 pieces. Halve plums, discard stones. Combine apples, rind, sugar, maple syrup, water and cinnamon in large pan, stir over low heat, without boiling, until sugar is dissolved. Bring to boil, simmer, uncovered, about 10 minutes or until apples are just tender, stirring occasionally.

2 Drain apples, discard cinnamon and syrup; cool. Combine apples, plums and nuts in bowl; mix gently.

3 Layer pastry sheets together, spraying every second sheet with cooking-oil spray. Spoon apple mixture along long edge of pastry, leaving 8cm border at each end. Roll up strudel, tucking in ends while rolling, coat lightly with cooking oil spray.

4 Place strudel on oven tray which has been coated with cooking-oil spray, bake in moderate oven about 30 minutes or until browned. Serve dusted with sifted icing sugar and candied lemon rind, if desired. Serve with vanilla yogurt.

Vanilla yogurt Combine all ingredients in bowl; mix well.

SERVES 6

Strudel and vanilla yogurt can be prepared a day ahead
Storage Covered, separately, in refrigerator
Freeze Not suitable
Microwave Not suitable
Diabetic Not suitable
Per serve fat 6.4g; 1280kJ

pavlovas with fresh berries

PREPARATION TIME 35 MINUTES • COOKING TIME 1 HOUR

3 egg whites
³/4 cup (165g) caster sugar
1 teaspoon vanilla essence
200g carton low-fat vanilla
**   fromage frais**
500g fresh berries
icing sugar

1 Cover oven tray with baking paper, mark four 8cm circles on paper. Beat egg whites in small bowl with electric mixer until soft peaks form. Gradually add sugar, beating until dissolved between additions, fold in essence.

2 Spread a rounded tablespoon of meringue mixture over each circle. Spoon remaining mixture into piping bag fitted with medium fluted tube. Pipe around edge of each round.

3 Bake in very slow oven about 1 hour or until pavlovas are dry and crisp. Divide fromage frais between pavlovas, top with half the berries. Dust with icing sugar, if desired. Blend or process remaining berries until smooth, serve with pavlovas.

SERVES 4

Recipe can be prepared a day ahead
Assemble just before serving

Storage Pavlovas, airtight container.

Freeze Not suitable

Diabetic Not suitable

Per serve fat 0.2g; 224kJ

orange and raspberry jellies

PREPARATION TIME 35 MINUTES (PLUS REFRIGERATION TIME)

ORANGE JELLY

1/2 cup (125ml) water

1/4 cup (55g) caster sugar

1 cup (250ml) orange juice

2 tablespoons Cointreau or Grand Marnier

2 tablespoons gelatine

1/4 cup (60ml) water, extra

RASPBERRY JELLY

3/4 cup (180ml) water

1/3 cup (75g) caster sugar

11/2 cups (185g) raspberries

2 tablespoons Bacardi rum

200g carton low-fat vanilla fromage frais

1 Line two 3-cup (750ml) dishes with plastic. Combine water and sugar in small pan, stir over heat, without boiling, until sugar is dissolved. Remove from heat, stir in juice and liqueur.

2 Sprinkle gelatine over extra water in cup, stand in small pan of simmering water, stir until dissolved, cool 5 minutes.

3 Add half the gelatine mixture to the orange mixture, pour into one of the prepared dishes; refrigerate until set.

Raspberry jelly Combine water and sugar in small pan, stir over heat, without boiling, until sugar

is dissolved, remove from heat. Process raspberries and sugar syrup until smooth, push mixture through a fine sieve into a medium bowl. Add rum, raspberry mixture and remaining gelatine mixture, pour into prepared dish; refrigerate until set.

SERVES 4

Serve jellies with fromage frais.

Storage Jellies, covered in refrigerator
Freeze Not suitable
Microwave Gelatine suitable

Diabetic Not suitable
Per serve fat 0.4g; 1164kJ

ricotta pancakes

PREPARATION TIME 20 MINUTES • COOKING TIME 15 MINUTES

1 cup (150g) white
self-raising flour
1 cup (160g) wholemeal
self-raising flour
1/3 cup (75g) caster sugar
1 cup (200g) low-fat
ricotta cheese
1 1/2 cups (375ml) low-fat milk
2 egg whites
cooking-oil spray

1 Sift flours and sugar into large bowl, whisk in cheese and milk. Beat egg whites in small bowl until soft peaks form, fold into ricotta mixture.

2 Place 1/2 cup (125ml) of mixture into non-stick pan which has been coated with cooking-oil spray, spread to 14cm round, cook over low heat until browned on both sides. Repeat with remaining mixture. You will need 8 pancakes for this recipe.

3 Serve pancakes with a tablespoon of maple-flavoured syrup, fresh berries and 2 small scoops of low-fat ice-cream per person.

SERVES 4

Recipe best made close to serving

Freeze Suitable
Microwave Not suitable

Diabetic Not suitable
Per serve fat 11.6g; 2525kJ

crepes with vanilla cream and raspberries

PREPARATION TIME 15 MINUTES (PLUS STANDING TIME) • COOKING TIME 15 MINUTES

3/4 cup (105g) plain flour
1 tablespoon caster sugar or
powdered artificial sweetener
1/2 teaspoon ground ginger
1 egg
1 1/4 cups (310ml) low-fat milk
cooking-oil spray
100g raspberries

VANILLA CREAM

50g packaged low-fat
cream cheese
2 tablespoons low-fat
sour cream
2 teaspoons icing sugar
mixture or powdered
artificial sweetener
1 teaspoon vanilla essence

1 Sift flour, sugar and ginger into bowl, gradually stir in combined egg and milk; beat until smooth. Cover, stand 30 minutes.

2 Pour 1/4 cup (60ml) batter into heated crepe pan which has been coated with cooking-oil spray; cook until lightly browned underneath. Turn crepe, brown other side. Repeat with remaining batter. You will need 8 crepes for this recipe.

3 Serve crepes with vanilla cream and raspberries.

Vanilla cream Combine all ingredients in bowl; mix well.

SERVES 4

Recipe can be made a day ahead

Storage Crepes and vanilla cream, covered, separately, in refrigerator
Freeze Crepes suitable
Microwave Not suitable

Diabetic Suitable for occasional use
Per serve fat 8.8g; 1045kJ

crepes with vanilla cream and raspberries *(back)*
ricotta pancakes *(right)*

fresh figs and dates in saffron syrup

PREPARATION TIME 25 MINUTES (PLUS COOLING TIME) • COOKING TIME 30 MINUTES

3/4 cup (180ml) water
1 cup (250ml) dry white wine
1/2 cup (110g) caster sugar
5cm piece orange rind
pinch saffron threads
1 cinnamon stick
**12 medium (600g) fresh
   figs, halved**
8 seedless fresh dates

CRISP BISCUITS

30g soft butter or margarine
1/4 cup (55g) caster sugar
1 egg white
2 1/2 tablespoons plain flour
cooking-oil spray

1 Combine water, wine and sugar in medium pan, stir over heat, without boiling, until sugar is dissolved. Add rind, saffron and cinnamon, simmer 15 minutes, strain; discard cinnamon, rind and threads.

2 Add figs to saffron syrup, boil, uncovered, about 3 minutes or until syrup is thickened slightly. Remove from heat, add dates, cover; cool. Serve with crisp biscuits.

Crisp biscuits Beat butter, sugar and egg white in small bowl with electric mixer on low speed until smooth and changed in colour, stir in sifted flour. Spoon mixture into piping bag fitted with 5mm plain tube. Pipe 8cm lengths onto oven trays which have been sprayed with cooking-oil spray; make biscuits slightly wider at both ends. Allow 6 biscuits per tray. Tap tray on bench to make biscuits spread slightly. Bake in hot oven about 5 minutes or until edges are browned. Lift onto wire racks to cool.

SERVES 4

Recipe can be made a day ahead

Storage Fruits in saffron syrup, covered, in refrigerator
Crisp biscuits, in airtight container
Freeze Not suitable
Microwave Not suitable

Diabetic Not suitable
Per serve fat 7.5g; 2170kJ

zucchini and kumara cake

PREPARATION TIME 35 MINUTES • COOKING TIME 50 MINUTES (PLUS COOLING TIME)

cooking-oil spray

3 eggs

¹/₂ cup (100g) firmly packed brown sugar

¹/₂ cup (75g) self-raising flour

2 teaspoons ground ginger

¹/₃ cup (40g) packaged ground almonds

10g butter or margarine, melted

1 tablespoon boiling water

¹/₂ cup (70g) finely grated zucchini

¹/₂ cup (65g) finely grated uncooked kumara

TOPPING

1 large (150g) zucchini

¹/₂ small (125g) kumara

¹/₂ cup (110g) caster sugar

¹/₃ cup (80ml) water

1 Coat deep 20cm round cake pan with cooking-oil spray, line base and side with baking paper.

2 Beat eggs and sugar in medium bowl with electric mixer until thick and creamy. Gently fold in sifted flour and ginger, nuts, butter and water. Fold in zucchini and kumara.

3 Spread mixture into prepared pan, bake in moderately hot oven about 35 minutes. Serve cake dusted with a little sifted icing sugar and decorated with topping, if desired.

Topping Peel zucchini thickly, cut skin into thin strips (remaining zucchini flesh is not used in this recipe).

Cut kumara into thin strips. Combine sugar and water in small pan, stir over heat, without boiling, until sugar is dissolved. Add zucchini and kumara, simmer, uncovered, 10 minutes; remove from syrup, cool on tray.

SERVES 8

Cake can be made a day ahead

Storage Airtight container
Freeze Cake suitable
Microwave Not suitable

Diabetic Not suitable
Per serve fat 6.3g; 935kJ

strawberry almond tart

PREPARATION TIME 40 MINUTES (PLUS CHILLING TIME) • COOKING TIME 20 MINUTES

1¼ cups (185g)
  self-raising flour
⅓ cup (40g) packaged
  ground almonds
2 tablespoons caster sugar
30g butter or margarine
½ cup (125ml) low-fat
  sour cream
cooking-oil spray
500g strawberries, halved
2 tablespoons apricot jam,
  warmed, sieved

FILLING

¾ cup (150g) low-fat
  ricotta cheese
200g carton low-fat vanilla
  fromage frais
2 tablespoons icing
  sugar mixture
½ teaspoon grated
  orange rind

1 Sift flour, nuts and sugar into bowl, rub in butter (or process flour, nuts, sugar and butter until mixture resembles breadcrumbs). Add cream, mix until ingredients cling together (or process until ingredients just come together). Press dough into a ball, knead gently on lightly floured surface until smooth, wrap in plastic, refrigerate 30 minutes.

2 Roll pastry between sheets of baking paper until large enough to line 24cm round loose-base flan tin which has been coated with cooking-oil spray. Lift pastry into tin, ease into side, trim edge. Prick base with fork and refrigerate 30 minutes.

3 Cover pastry with baking paper, fill with dried beans or rice; place on oven tray, bake in moderately hot oven 10 minutes. Remove paper and beans carefully from pastry case, bake further 10 minutes or until browned; cool.

4 Spread filling into pastry case, top with strawberries, brush with jam.

Filling Combine all ingredients in bowl; mix well.

SERVES 8

Recipe can be made a day ahead

Storage Covered, in refrigerator
Freeze Not suitable
Microwave Not suitable

Diabetic Not suitable
Per serve fat 10.9g; 1100kJ

spicy baked apples

PREPARATION TIME 25 MINUTES • COOKING TIME 35 MINUTES

4 medium (600g) apples
20g soft butter or margarine
1/4 cup (50g) brown sugar
2 teaspoons rosewater
1/2 teaspoon ground cinnamon
pinch ground cardamom
1 tablespoon pine
  nuts, toasted
2 tablespoons shelled
  pistachios, toasted, chopped
1/4 cup (35g) dried currants
1 tablespoon chopped
  dried apricots
1 tablespoon chopped
  dried figs

HONEY FROMAGE FRAIS

2 teaspoons rosewater
200g carton low-fat vanilla fromage frais
2 teaspoons honey

1 Remove cores and slit skin of each apple around centre. Cut shallow 3cm hole in top of each apple. Combine remaining ingredients in small bowl; mix well. Spoon mixture into each apple cavity.

2 Place apples in large ovenproof dish, bake, covered, in moderately hot oven about 35 minutes or until apples are tender.

3 Serve with pan juices and honey fromage frais.

   Honey fromage frais Combine all ingredients in small bowl; mix well.

SERVES 4

Recipe best made just before serving

Freeze Not suitable
Microwave Suitable

Diabetic Not suitable
Per serve fat 12.9g; 1195kJ

quinces on cinnamon orange polenta

PREPARATION TIME 35 MINUTES (PLUS COOLING TIME) • COOKING TIME 2 HOURS

2 small (550g) quinces,
    peeled, quartered, cored
$1/4$ cup (55g) caster
    sugar or powdered
    artificial sweetener
$1/2$ cup (125ml) water
$1/4$ cup (20g) flaked
    almonds, toasted

CINNAMON ORANGE POLENTA

$1 1/2$ cups (375ml) water
$1/2$ cup (50g) low-fat
    milk powder
2 teaspoons grated
    orange rind
1 teaspoon ground cinnamon
2 tablespoons caster
    sugar or powdered
    artificial sweetener
$1/2$ cup (85g) polenta
cooking-oil spray

RICOTTA CREAM

1 cup (200g) low-fat
    ricotta cheese, sieved
$1/4$ cup (40g) icing sugar
    mixture or powdered
    artificial sweetener
1 teaspoon ground cinnamon
1 teaspoon grated
    orange rind
2 tablespoons low-fat milk

1 Cut quince quarters into 4 slices, slightly overlap in 19cm x 29cm rectangular slice pan, sprinkle with sugar, add water. Cover pan tightly with foil.

2 Bake in moderately hot oven about $1 1/4$ hours or until quinces are tender. Drain syrup from quinces into small pan, cook, uncovered, until reduced to about 2 tablespoons. Place 8 slices of quince on each polenta base, brush with a little of the syrup, sprinkle with nuts. Serve with ricotta cream.

Cinnamon orange polenta
Combine water, milk powder, rind, cinnamon and sugar in medium pan, bring to boil, add polenta, cook, stirring about 8 minutes or until mixture is very thick; cool 5 minutes. Divide mixture into 4 portions, roll each portion into a ball,

using damp hands; flatten to 10cm rounds on oven tray sprayed with cooking-oil spray. Bake in moderately hot oven 15 minutes, turn bases over, bake further 15 minutes or until browned and crisp.

Ricotta cream Combine all ingredients in bowl; mix well.

SERVES 4

Polenta and ricotta cream can be made a day ahead

Storage Covered, separately, in refrigerator
Freeze Not suitable
Microwave Not suitable

Diabetic Suitable for occasional use
Per serve fat 7.9g; 1550kJ

banana and carob chip ice-cream

PREPARATION TIME 15 MINUTES (PLUS FREEZING TIME)

You will need 3 medium (600g) overripe bananas for this recipe

**1 cup (250ml) low-fat
    evaporated milk**
1 cup mashed bananas
**1/2 cup (125ml)
    low-fat yogurt**
1/4 cup (60ml) low-fat milk
**1/4 cup (60ml) maple-
    flavoured syrup**
2 teaspoons vanilla essence
**1/3 cup (50g) carob
    buttons, chopped**

1 Pour evaporated milk into loaf
  pan, cover with foil, freeze until
  just firm. Process evaporated
  milk, bananas, yogurt, milk,
  maple syrup and essence until
  thick and creamy.

2 Pour mixture into 15cm x 25cm
  loaf pan, cover, freeze until just
  firm. Repeat processing, stir in
  carob, cover, freeze until firm.

SERVES 4

*Ice-cream can be made
a week ahead*

Storage Covered, in freezer

Diabetic Suitable
Per serve fat 3.5g; 970kJ

apple and date meringue pie

PREPARATION TIME 30 MINUTES (PLUS COOLING TIME) • COOKING TIME 30 MINUTES (PLUS COOLING TIME)

cooking-oil spray
30g butter
2 tablespoons caster sugar
1¹/₂ cups (225g) self-raising
  flour
2 tablespoons custard powder
¹/₃ cup (80ml) low-fat
  evaporated milk,
  approximately

FILLING

4 large (800g) apples,
  peeled, chopped
1 cup (250ml) apple juice
¹/₂ teaspoon ground cinnamon
1 tablespoon caster sugar
10 (230g) seedless fresh
  dates, roughly chopped
1 tablespoon cornflour
1 tablespoon water

MERINGUE

3 egg whites
²/₃ cup (150g) caster sugar

1 Coat 24cm round loose-base flan tin with cooking-oil spray.

2 Process butter, sugar, flour and custard powder until combined. Add enough milk to make ingredients just come together. Knead on floured surface until smooth, wrap in plastic, refrigerate 30 minutes.

3 Roll dough on floured surface until large enough to line prepared tin. Lift pastry into tin, ease into side, trim edge. Cover pastry with baking paper, fill with dried beans or rice, place on oven tray.

4 Bake in moderately hot oven 10 minutes, remove paper and beans carefully from pastry case, bake further 5 minutes or until browned; cool.

5 Spoon filling into pastry case, top with meringue. Bake in moderate oven about 5 minutes or until lightly browned.

Filling Combine apples, juice, cinnamon and sugar in large pan, bring to boil, simmer, uncovered, until apples are just tender. Add dates, cook, stirring, 1 minute. Add blended cornflour and water, stir until mixture boils and thickens; cool.

Meringue Beat egg whites in small bowl with electric mixer until soft peaks form, gradually add sugar, beating until dissolved between additions.

SERVES 8

Pastry case can be made a day ahead; recipe best assembled just before serving

Storage Pastry case, in airtight container
Freeze Uncooked pastry suitable
Microwave Filling suitable
Diabetic Not suitable
Per serve fat 3.6g; 1640kJ

pear and rhubarb crumble

PREPARATION TIME 20 MINUTES • COOKING TIME 25 MINUTES

2³/₄ cups (300g) chopped
  fresh rhubarb
2 tablespoons caster sugar
¹/₂ cup (125ml) water
¹/₄ cup (60ml) orange juice
8 medium (1.4kg) pears,
  peeled, chopped
³/₄ cup (120g) chopped raisins

CRUMBLE TOPPING

1 cup (30g) corn flakes
¹/₂ cup (55g) natural muesli

25g butter, melted
2 tablespoons honey

1 Combine rhubarb, sugar, water, juice and pears in pan, bring to boil, simmer, uncovered, until pears are just tender. Stir in raisins.

2 Spoon mixture into ovenproof dish (1.5 lite/6 cup), sprinkle with crumble topping.

3 Bake in moderate oven about 15 minutes or until browned.

Crumble topping Combine corn flakes and muesli in bowl, add butter and honey; mix well.

SERVES 8

Recipe best made close to serving

Freeze Not suitable
Microwave Not suitable
Diabetic Suitable
Per serve fat 3.3g; 885kJ

apple and date meringue pie *(back)*
pear and rhubarb crumble *(right)*

low fat – not no fat!

You don't have to give up fat altogether – just reduce your intake, and still enjoy eating!

Eating less fat (and less saturated fat, in particular) is one of the best things you can do for your health and your body shape. Gram for gram, fat packs in more kilojoules than either carbohydrate or protein. So 10 grams of pure fat supplies 370 kilojoules, while 10 grams of pure carbohydrate or protein has only 170 kilojoules.

Low-fat foods such as potatoes, rice, pasta, vegetables, fruit, breads, cereals and beans are naturally low in fat only if fats are not added in cooking or processing. For example, some people consider instant noodles low in fat, but they are actually high in fat due to processing. Low fat foods are filling, nutritious foods that are less likely to add weight. However, take care if you add extra fats, such as butter or sour cream, or by frying.

Years ago, people often avoided starchy foods, such as bread and potatoes, in the belief that they were "fattening". But metabolic studies over the past 15 years have shown that carbohydrates are not readily converted to body fat, but instead are burned off (oxidised). On the other

hand, fats are less likely to be oxidised and are efficiently stored as body fat. It is chemically easier for the body to turn food fat into body fat than to break down carbohydrate and re-form it as fat.

Carbohydrates make us feel full more quickly than fat. We need to eat carbohydrate because it is an essential fuel for the brain, liver and muscles. Eating carbohydrate at each meal helps to satisfy hunger and meets our energy needs with less risk of weight gain. So a low-fat, high-carbohydrate diet is part of the secret behind better weight control.

Fat and disease

High intakes of saturated fat have been linked to illnesses, such as coronary heart disease, mature-age diabetes and certain types of cancer, notably cancer of the bowel and the breast. Cutting back on saturated fat and substituting small quantities of unsaturated fats and oils is part of the dietary strategy to ward off these problems. The recipes in this book show you how to create low-fat dishes that are healthy and delicious. All are also low in saturated fat so would be suitable to reduce blood cholesterol levels or lessen the risk of future illness.

1 250ml skim milk = 0.03g fat
2 250ml full-cream milk = 9.89g fat
3 300g pouring full cream = 120g fat
4 200g carton sour cream = 79g fat
5 5g butter = 4g fat
6 5g diet polyunsaturated reduced fat spread = 2g fat
7 200g low-fat yogurt = 0.4g fat

Comparisons from the dairy

Which one of these pairs has the lower fat content?

50g potato chips = 16.1g fat
50g pretzels = 4g fat

20g jam = 0.01g fat
20g peanut butter = 10.5g fat

100g fillo pastry = 3g fat
100g puff pastry = 26g fat

100g toffee-nut ice-cream = 13g fat
100g lemon sorbet = 1.4g fat

Fat is fine in small amounts

A small amount of fat is essential for good health, vitality and clear skin. Children, especially, need some fat in their meals to grow and develop properly. A low-fat diet is not recommended for young children under the age of 5 years.

Fat acts as a carrier for fat-soluble vitamins (vitamins A, D, E and K) and also supplies two essential fatty acids. Known as linoleic acid and alpha-linolenic acid, these polyunsaturated fatty acids cannot be made in the body and so must come from food. They are needed to maintain the structure of cell membranes and to form a series of hormone-like substances that regulate much of the body's biochemistry.

The minimum amount of fat required to prevent essential fatty acid deficiency is 10g. Essential fatty acids can be found in foods such as vegetable oils, grains, nuts, seeds, wheatgerm and fish oils.

Beware of potato toppings

1 medium (150g) plain baked potato = 0g fat
2 2 tablespoons guacamole = 8g fat
3 2 tablespoons sour cream = 7g fat
4 salsa = 0g fat

How much fat do I need?

WOMEN The recommended intake of fat is 50 to 60 grams a day for moderately active women aged 18 to 54 years. This is based on 30 per cent of kilojoules being derived from fat. Very active women can eat a little more fat – around 70 to 80 grams a day.

MEN Men should also aim for 70 to 80 grams a day if they are fairly active, or 80 to 100 grams if they do lots of physical activity.

Weight control

If you are overweight, keeping your fat intake to only 30 to 50 grams a day is a sensible and easy way to shed excess body fat.

How to check fat grams

Buy an inexpensive fat counter, available at bookshops or chemists. As well, the nutrition information on food labels includes the amount of fat in individual products.

fat facts

NEGLIGIBLE
Virtually no fat

Alcoholic drinks
Baked beans
Crabs, lobsters, prawns, cooked without fat
Egg whites
Fruit juices
Fruit, fresh, canned, stewed or dried
Jams, marmalades, chutneys
Legumes (beans, peas, lentils)
Mineral waters, soft drinks, cordials
Noodles, boiled (not instant)
No-oil salad dressings, vinegars
Pasta, boiled
Potatoes, boiled or baked in jacket
Rice, white, steamed or boiled
Skim milk
Skim milk powder
Sugar, honey, golden syrup
Vegetable juices (carrot, celery, tomato, etc)
Vegetables, raw, steamed, boiled or dry-baked (except for olives and avocados)
Yeast spreads

LOW
Less than 3 per cent fat

Bread, all varieties
Breakfast cereals (excluding muesli)
Crispbreads
Fruit loaves
Gelatos, sorbets
Low-fat and reduced-fat milks
Low-fat soy beverages
Most white fish, grilled or steamed
Muffins, crumpets
Oysters, scallops, squid
Popcorn, plain
Rice, brown, steamed or boiled
Rolled oats (porridge)
Yogurt, low-fat

MEDIUM
3 to 20 per cent fat

Biscuits, plain sweet*
Cakes, plain uniced*
Cottage cheese, farm cheese
Cracker biscuits*
Egg yolks*
Fillo pastry
Fish fingers, fried
Full-cream milk powder*
Full-cream milk, goats milk*
Hot potato chips*
Lean beef, trim lamb, veal, chicken, new-fashioned pork (grilled or cooked without fat)
Muesli, Swiss-style

Muesli, toasted*
Oily fish, grilled, steamed or baked without fat
Olives, garlic, mashed potato with milk and butter
Pretzels
Rice bran
Salmon, tuna, fresh (grilled or steamed) and canned
Sardines, canned in oil
Scones, fruit buns, pancakes, pikelets
Smoked salmon
Soy beverages
Venison, kangaroo and other game meat, cooked without fat
Wheat bran, oat bran

HIGH
21 to 50 per cent fat

Avocados
Biscuits, cream-filled and shortbread types*
Cakes, rich and cream-filled types*
Chocolate*
Coconut cream*, coconut milk*
Corn chips*
Cream*
Croissants*, garlic bread*
Delicatessen meats*, salami*
Doughnuts*
Fried foods*, crumbed chicken*, fried fish pieces*
Fried rice
Hard cheeses*, cream cheese*
Pan-fried bacon*
Pastry*
Potato crisps, cheese-flavoured snacks*
Sausages*, rissoles*, fatty meats*

VERY HIGH
Over 50 per cent fat

Butter*
Copha (hardened coconut fat)*
Desiccated coconut*
Lard*, dripping*
Margarine, table and cooking*
Nuts
Olive oil, all types including light olive oil
Oils, polyunsaturated and mono-unsaturated
Peanut butters, nut butters
Reduced-fat margarines
Seeds (sesame, sunflower, pumpkin, etc)

* Means the fat in that food is mostly saturated. Most commercial foods (such as cakes, biscuits, fried foods etc) contain largely saturated fats, but home-cooked versions could be made with mono-unsaturated or polyunsaturated oils or margarines.

Types of fat in food

SATURATED FATS tend to be solid and are found mainly in animal products, such as butter, cream, fat on meat, chicken skin, cheese, lard and dripping. Palm and coconut oils – vegetable oils used in food manufacture and for deep-frying – are also mainly saturated. Bought foods, such as biscuits, cakes, pies, pastries and snack foods, also tend to be high in saturates. Saturated fats tend to raise blood cholesterol (although the extent to which they do this varies) and they have been incriminated in many illnesses. They are the fats to avoid. Concentrate on the polyunsaturated and mono-unsaturated fats.

TRANS FATTY ACIDS are hydrogenated forms of polyunsaturated or mono-unsaturated fatty acids that can raise LDL-cholesterol (the "bad" form of cholesterol) to the same degree as do saturated fats.

Trans fats have a different configuration of atoms and so behave biologically as if they were saturated. Humans have been consuming trans fatty acids for centuries, as they occur in butter, milk, beef and lamb. They are also formed during the manufacture of margarine,

when liquid vegetable oils are hydrogenated (hardened) to turn them into solids.

Although still under research, most authorities consider trans fats similar to saturated fats, and recommend limiting their intake.

POLYUNSATURATED FATS are generally oils at room temperature. They are found in nuts and grains and are extracted from seeds, such as sunflower, safflower, soy bean, cottonseed, maize (corn), sesame and grape seed. Oily fish (herring, salmon, tuna, mackerel and sardines) and seafood contain highly polyunsaturated fats, known as omega-3 fatty acids.

Polyunsaturated fats lessen the fatty build-up on artery walls and reduce cholesterol in the blood – but we only need small quantities.

MONO-UNSATURATED FATS predominate in olives, olive oil, canola oil, peanuts, peanut oil, avocados, macadamias and hazelnuts. All vegetable oils contain mono-unsaturates in varying amounts, as do lean meats, chicken, eggs and fish. Mono-fats were once considered "neutral", meaning that they neither raised nor lowered cholesterol. Today, however, they feature in diets for a healthy heart.

100g **sea mullet** = 2359mg omega-3

100g John Dory = 200mg omega-3

100g **snapper** = 450mg omega-3

100g **silver bream** = 200mg omega-3

The good oil

LITE or LIGHT does not always mean that a food is low in kilojoules or fat. Light potato crisps, for example, are lightly salted and thinly sliced, but still have about the same amount of fat as other crisps; light beer is low in alcohol; light olive oil has a lighter flavour but the same amount of fat as regular olive oil.

97 PER CENT FAT-FREE really means that the food contains 3 per cent fat, but the wording makes it sound better for you than it actually is.

CHOLESTEROL FREE or NO CHOLESTEROL can be confusing, as it is frequently taken to mean no fat. Many foods, such as nuts, olives, peanut butter, oils, margarines, sauces and avocados, are free of cholesterol but remain high in fat. They are only suitable for you if they are also low in fat *or* low in saturated fat (check the label). Cholesterol occurs in foods of animal origin, so food made from plants is automatically free of cholesterol. Fat content, particularly saturated fat, is more important to reduce than cholesterol.

COOKED IN VEGETABLE OIL does not always mean the oil is polyunsaturated or mono-unsaturated. The most common oil used to fry snacks and fast foods is palm oil, a tropical oil which is 50 per cent saturated. While it qualifies as a vegetable oil, it differs greatly from the unsaturated vegetable oils, such as canola, soy bean and sunflower oil. If one of these oils is in the food, it will usually tell you on the pack. If not, you can assume it is palm oil or trans fatty acids, a type of saturated fat.

REDUCED-FAT foods contain less fat than regular products, but may not necessarily be low in fat. Usually, there is 25 per cent less fat than in the regular counterpart.

POLYUNSATURATED on the label of margarines, spreads, mayonnaise, oils, salad dressings and biscuits is often perceived to mean low in fat and, therefore, non-fattening. The truth is that all fats supply the same number of kilojoules, regardless of whether they are polyunsaturated, mono-unsaturated or saturated. For instance, butter, margarine and dairy blends all have the same kilojoule count, and coconut oil (a saturated oil) has the same as safflower oil (polyunsaturated).

KILOJOULES OR CALORIES? Kilojoules are the metric equivalent of calories. To convert to calories, divide kilojoules by 4.186 or simply by 4. For example, a slice of bread at 250 kilojoules is equivalent to 60 calories.

glossary

Angostura aromatic bitters
Angostura is a brand name for a type of bitters. It is based on rum, infused with bitter aromatic bark, herbs and spices.

Arrowroot Used mostly for thickening.

Bacardi Clear rum from Puerto Rico.

Bacon rashers Bacon slices.

Baking powder Raising agent consisting of a starch, but mostly cream of tartar and bicarbonate of soda in the proportions of 1 level teaspoon cream of tartar to 1/2 level teaspoon bicarbonate of soda. This is equivalent to 2 teaspoons baking powder.

Bean mix (4-bean mix)
Canned mix of red kidney, garbanzo (chickpeas), baby lima and butter beans.

Bean sprouts Also known as bean shoots. We used soy bean sprouts.

Beef
EYE FILLET Tenderloin.
NEW YORK CUT STEAK Sirloin without T-bone.
RUMP STEAK Boneless piece of meat that covers the hip bone.

Beetroot Red beets.

Bicarbonate of soda
Baking soda.

Breadcrumbs
PACKAGED Use fine packaged breadcrumbs.
STALE Use 1- or 2-day-old bread made into crumbs by grating, blending or processing.

Burghul Hulled wheat that is steamed until partly cooked, dried, then crushed into various size grains. Cracked wheat can be substituted; also known as bulghur wheat.

Butter Use salted or unsalted (also called sweet) butter; 125g is equal to 1 stick butter.

Buttermilk Made by adding a culture to low-fat milk to give a slightly acidic flavour. A low-fat yogurt can be substituted.

Butternut pumpkin Pear-shaped with golden skin and orange flesh; also known as butternut squash.

Cajun seasoning
Combination of dried ingredients consisting of salt, capsicum, garlic, onion and spices.

Calamari Squid.

Capsicum Bell peppers.

Carob buttons Chocolate substitutes.

Cayenne pepper Variety of chilli, often dried and ground into a hot, red-brown powder.

Chickpeas Garbanzos.

Chillies Available in many types and sizes. Use rubber gloves when chopping chillies as they can burn your skin.
DRIED, CRUSHED available from supermarkets and Asian food stores.
SWEET CHILLI SAUCE Mild Thai-style sauce made from red chillies, sugar, garlic, salt and vinegar.

Choko Also known as chayote or christophenes. A pear-shaped vegetable with a pale green skin.

Cocoa Cocoa powder.

Cointreau Orange-flavoured liqueur.

Cornflour Cornstarch.

Couscous Fine, grain-like cereal made from semolina.

Creme de Cassis
Blackcurrant-flavoured liqueur.

Cream of tartar the acid ingredient in baking powder; added to confectionery mixtures to help prevent sugar crystallising. Keeps frostings creamy and improves volume when beating egg whites.

Curry paste We used bottled curry pastes available from supermarkets and Asian food stores.

Curry powder Combination of powdered spices including chilli, coriander, cumin, fennel, fenugreek and turmeric.

Custard powder A thickening powder for making custard without eggs.

Drinking chocolate
Sweetened cocoa powder.

Eggplant Aubergine.

Essence Extract.

Fennel Has a slight aniseed taste when fresh, ground or in seed form. The bulb can be eaten uncooked in salads, braised, steamed or stir-fried.

Fillo pastry Also known as phyllo dough; comes in tissue-thin pastry sheets bought chilled or frozen.

Fish sauce Made from the liquid drained from salted, fermented anchovies. Has a strong smell and taste; use sparingly. The intensity of flavour varies. We used Thai fish sauce.

Five-spice powder Pungent mixture of ground spices which include cinnamon, cloves, fennel, star anise and Sichuan pepper.

Flour
BUCKWHEAT Although not a true cereal, flour is made from its seeds. Available from health food stores.
LENTIL Available from health food stores.
WHITE PLAIN Unbleached all-purpose flour.
WHITE SELF-RAISING Substitute plain (all-purpose) flour and baking powder in the proportions of 1 cup (150g) plain flour to 2 level teaspoons baking powder. Sift together several times before using.
WHOLEMEAL PLAIN Wholewheat flour without the addition of baking powder.
WHOLEMEAL SELF-RAISING Wholewheat flour with baking powder added.

Focaccia Leavened, flat Italian-style bread.

Frangelico Hazelnut-flavoured liqueur.

Garam masala Combination of ground spices, consisting of cardamom, cinnamon, cloves, coriander, cumin and nutmeg in varying proportions. Sometimes pepper is used to make a hot variation.

Golden syrup Maple, pancake syrup or honey can be substituted.

Gow gee wrappers Wonton wrappers, spring roll or egg pastry sheets can be substituted.

Grand Marnier An orange-flavoured liqueur.

Hoisin sauce A thick, sweet, spicy Chinese paste made from salted, fermented black beans, onion and garlic.

Jalapeño chillies Hot chillies, available in brine in bottles and cans.

Jam Conserve or preserve.

Kiwi fruit also known as Chinese gooseberry.

Kumara Orange-fleshed sweet potato.

Lamb
EYE OF LOIN A cut derived from a row of loin chops. Once the bone and fat are removed, the larger portion is referred to as the eye of the loin.
FILLET Tenderloin; the smaller piece of meat from a row of loin chops or cutlets.
MINCED Ground lamb.
TRIM LAMB Boneless cuts, free from any external fat.

Lamington pan 20cm x 30cm slab cake pan, 3cm deep.

semolina
couscous
barley
polenta
burghul
felafel mix

Lemon grass Lemon-tasting grass; lower white part of stem is used in Asian cooking.

Maple-flavoured syrup Golden or pancake syrup; honey can also be substituted.

Midori melon liqueur Green, honey-dew melon-flavoured liqueur.

Muesli Also known as Granola.

Mustard, seeded French-style textured mustard with crushed mustard seeds.

Noodles
EGG Made from wheat, flour and eggs; varying in thickness from fine strands to as thick as a shoelace.
FLAT RICE Fresh soft white rice-flour noodles.

Oat bran Layer under the oat husk.

Ocean trout Farmed fish with pink, soft flesh; from same family as Atlantic salmon.

Oyster sauce Asian in origin, a rich brown sauce made from oysters and their brine; cooked in salt and soy sauce, then thickened with starches.

Pasta
ANGEL'S HAIR Very fine, also known as capelli d'angelo.
BUCKWHEAT Pasta made from buckwheat flour; also called soba noodles.
RISONI Rice-shaped pasta.
TORTELLINI Small pieces of pasta, filled, sealed, then shaped into rounds.
WHOLEMEAL LASAGNE SHEETS Lasagne sheets made from wholemeal and white flour.

Pearl barley Barley with its outer husk removed, then steamed and polished.

Pepitas Dried pumpkin seeds.

Polenta Ground corn (maize); similar to cornmeal but coarser and darker in colour. Also, the dish made from it.

Pork
AMERICAN-STYLE SPARE RIBS Well-trimmed mid-loin ribs.
BUTTERFLY Skinless, boneless mid-loin chop, split in half and flattened.
FILLET Skinless, boneless eye-fillet, cut from the loin.
STEAK Schnitzel; usually cut from the leg or rump.

Prawns Shrimp.

Prosciutto Salt-cured, air-dried, pressed pork; ready to eat when bought.

Quince Yellow-skinned fruit with hard texture and acid taste which cooks to a rich pink colour.

Redcurrant jelly Preserve made from redcurrants.

Rice paper rounds Translucent sheets made from rice flour. Dipped momentarily in water, they become pliable wrappers for fresh spring rolls. There is no substitute.

Rosewater Extract made from crushed rose petals.

Sake Japanese rice wine used in cooking, marinades, and dipping sauces. As a drink, served warm.

Saffron Available in strands or ground form; imparts an orange colour to food. Quality varies greatly.

Sambal oelek (also ulek or olek) Indonesian in origin, a salty paste made from ground chillies.

Seasoned Pepper Packaged preparation of black pepper, paprika, garlic and dried red capsicum.

Shallots
FRENCH SHALLOTS Very small onion with brown skin; grows in clusters, and has a strong onion and garlic flavour.
GREEN ONIONS Also known as scallions or spring onions.

Star anise
Dried star-shaped fruit of an evergreen tree; used sparingly in Chinese cooking. Has an aniseed flavour.

star anise

Sugar We used coarse granulated table sugar, also known as crystal sugar, unless otherwise specified.
BROWN Soft, fine granulated sugar containing molasses.
CASTER Also known as superfine; is fine granulated table sugar.
ICING Also known as confectioners' sugar or powdered sugar. We used icing sugar mixture, not icing sugar, unless specified.

Sichuan pepper (also known as Chinese pepper) Small, red-brown seeds resembling black peppercorns; they have a peppery-lemon flavour.

canned green peppercorns

Sichuan peppercorns

black peppercorns

Sultanas Seedless golden raisins.

Tabasco sauce Made with vinegar, hot red chillies and salt.

Tamarind sauce If unavailable, soak about 30g dried tamarind in a cup of hot water, stand 10 minutes, allow to cool, squeeze pulp until it is as dry as possible, then use the flavoured water.

Tequila Pale amber alcoholic liquor of Mexican origin made from the fermented sap of the agave, a succulent desert plant.

Teriyaki sauce Made of light Japanese soy sauce, sugar, spices and vinegar.

Tofu Made from boiled, crushed soy beans; also known as beancurd. We used firm and soft tofu in this book. Buy tofu as fresh as possible; keep any leftover tofu in the refrigerator under water, which must be changed daily.

Tomato
PASTE A concentrated tomato puree used in flavouring soups, stews, sauces and casseroles, etc.
PUREE Canned, pureed tomatoes (not tomato paste). Use fresh, peeled, pureed tomatoes as a substitute, if preferred.
SUPREME A canned product consisting of tomatoes, onions, celery, capsicum, cheese and seasonings.

Tortilla Thin, round, unleavened bread; can be bought or made at home – see how in our *Easy Mexican-Style Cookbook*.

Vanilla bean Dried bean of the vanilla orchid. It can be used repeatedly, simply wash in warm water after use, dry well and store in airtight container.

Veal
NUT OF VEAL Lean cut from the leg.
STEAK Schnitzel.

Vinegar
BALSAMIC Originated in the province of Modena, Italy. Regional wine is specially processed, then aged in antique wood casks to give a pungent flavour.
BROWN MALT Dark brown vinegar made from fermented malted barley and beech shavings.
RED WINE Based on red wine.
RICE Colourless seasoned vinegar made from fermented rice, sugar and salt.
WHITE Made from spirit of cane sugar.

Wheatgerm Small, creamy flakes milled from the embryo of the wheat.

Yeast Allow 2 teaspoons (7g) dried yeast to each 15g compressed yeast, if substituting one for the other.

Zucchini Courgette.

corn tortilla

flour tortilla

index

facts and figures

Wherever you live, you'll be able to use our recipes with the help of these easy-to-follow conversions. While they are approximate only, the slight differences will not affect your results.

how to measure
The difference between one country's measuring cups and another's is, at most, within a 2- or 3-teaspoon variance. (One Australian metric measuring cup holds approximately 250ml.) The most accurate way of measuring dry ingredients is to weigh them. When using graduated metric measuring cups, shake dry ingredients loosely into the appropriate cup. Do not tap cup on a bench or tightly pack the ingredients unless directed to do so. Level top of measuring cups and measuring spoons with a knife. When measuring liquids, place a clear glass or plastic jug with metric markings on a flat surface to check accuracy at eye level.

Note: North America, NZ and UK use 15ml tablespoons. All cup and spoon measurements are level.

We use large eggs having an average weight of 60g.

DRY MEASURES

metric	imperial
15g	1/2oz
30g	1oz
60g	2oz
90g	3oz
125g	4oz (1/4lb)
155g	5oz
185g	6oz
220g	7oz
250g	8oz (1/2lb)
280g	9oz
315g	10oz
345g	11oz
375g	12oz (3/4lb)
410g	13oz
440g	14oz
470g	15oz
500g	16oz (1lb)
750g	24oz (1 1/2lb)
1kg	32oz (2lb)

LIQUID MEASURES

metric	imperial
30ml	1 fluid oz
60ml	2 fluid oz
100ml	3 fluid oz
125ml	4 fluid oz
150ml	5 fluid oz (1/4 pint/1 gill)
190ml	6 fluid oz
250ml	8 fluid oz
300ml	10 fluid oz (1/2 pint)
500ml	16 fluid oz
600ml	20 fluid oz (1 pint)
1 litre	32 fluid oz (1 3/4 pints)

HELPFUL MEASURES

metric	imperial
3mm	1/8in
6mm	1/4in
1cm	1/2in
2cm	3/4in
2.5cm	1in
5cm	2in
6cm	2 1/2in
8cm	3in
10cm	4in
13cm	5in
15cm	6in
18cm	7in
20cm	8in
23cm	9in
25cm	10in
28cm	11in
30cm	12in (1ft)

OVEN TEMPERATURES

These oven temperatures are only a guide. Always check the manufacturer's manual.

	C° (Celsius)	F° (Fahrenheit)	Gas Mark
Very slow	120	250	1
Slow	150	300	2
Moderately slow	160	325	3
Moderate	180–190	350–375	4
Moderately hot	200–210	400–425	5
Hot	220–230	450–475	6
Very hot	240–250	500–525	7

low-fat stock

If you prefer to make your own stock, these recipes can be made up to 4 days ahead and stored, covered, in the refrigerator. Be sure to remove any fat from the surface after the cooled stock has been refrigerated overnight. If the stock is to be kept longer, it is best to freeze it in smaller quantities.

Stock is also available in cans or tetra packs. Be aware of their salt content. Stock cubes or powder can be used. As a guide, 1 teaspoon of stock powder or 1 small crumbled stock cube mixed with 1 cup (250ml) water will give a fairly strong stock. Be aware of the salt and fat content of stock cubes and powders.

BEEF STOCK
2kg meaty beef bones
2 medium (300g) onions
2 sticks celery, chopped
2 medium (250g) carrots, chopped
3 bay leaves
2 teaspoons black peppercorns
5 litres (20 cups) water
3 litres (12 cups) water, extra

Place bones and unpeeled chopped onions in baking dish. Bake in hot oven about 1 hour or until bones and onions are well browned. Transfer bones and onions to large pan, add celery, carrots, bay leaves, peppercorns and water, simmer, uncovered, 3 hours. Add extra water, simmer, uncovered, further 1 hour, strain.

MAKES ABOUT 2.5 LITRES (10 CUPS)

FISH STOCK
1.5kg fish bones
3 litres (12 cups) water
1 medium (150g) onion, chopped
2 sticks celery, chopped
2 bay leaves
1 teaspoon black peppercorns

Combine all ingredients in large pan, simmer, uncovered, 20 minutes; strain.

MAKES ABOUT 2.5 LITRES (10 CUPS)

CHICKEN STOCK
2kg chicken bones
2 medium (300g) onions, chopped
2 sticks celery, chopped
2 medium (250g) carrots, chopped
3 bay leaves
2 teaspoons black peppercorns
5 litres (20 cups) water

Combine all ingredients in large pan, simmer, uncovered, 2 hours; strain.

MAKES ABOUT 2.5 LITRES (10 CUPS)

VEGETABLE STOCK
1 large (180g) carrot, chopped
1 large (180g) parsnip, chopped
2 medium (300g) onions, chopped
6 sticks celery, chopped
4 bay leaves
2 teaspoons black peppercorns
3 litres (12 cups) water

Combine all ingredients in large pan, simmer, uncovered, 1 1/2 hours; strain.

MAKES ABOUT 1.25 LITRES (5 CUPS)

eating well with diabetes

People with diabetes can today select a wide variety of foods, aimed at reducing fats and sugar, and increasing fibre. Here we answer some of the most frequently-asked questions.

How important are regular meals? Blood glucose levels are easily managed if meals are evenly spaced. With irregular meals and serving sizes, blood sugars will be more difficult to control.

What about snacks? Not everyone with diabetes needs to eat between meals. Some people on diabetes medication (tablets or insulin) are encouraged to include snacks to prevent a drop in blood sugars. The best snacks are those low in fat and high in fibre, such as all types of fresh and dried fruit, low-fat fruit muffins, crumpets, low-fat muesli bars, low-fat yogurt, plain biscuits and crackers.

Why focus on saturated fats? A greater emphasis is now placed on reducing fat intake and promoting healthy blood vessels. Eating excess fat, no matter what type, promotes excess body fat but it's the saturated fat that's the biggest dietary cause of unhealthy blood vessels. Even if you're not over-weight, it's important to avoid large amounts of saturated fat.

How much fat can I eat? Guidelines on pages 112 to 114 apply equally if you have diabetes. If you are overweight and have diabetes, it is particularly important to lose excess weight. Control of blood glucose levels can improve significantly with small losses in weight. Aim to keep your fat intake between 40 to 50 grams (8 to 10 teaspoons) per day. For health reasons, it is preferable to select polyunsaturated and mono-unsaturated fats. These are found in safflower, sunflower, canola and olive-based margarines and oils, nuts, seeds, olives, fish and other seafood.

Why does each recipe have its fat value calculated? The fat counts enable you to keep within your daily range. Remember to count all sources of fat, such as spreads on breads, and so on.

Must I follow a sugar-free diet? No. Small amounts of sugar, as part of a low-fat, high-fibre meal, are not a problem. For this reason, recipes with sugar or honey in small amounts (less than 2 teaspoons per serve) are acceptable. However, sugar-rich foods are generally reserved for special occasions or eaten in small amounts only. Some recipes in the dessert section requiring large amounts of sugar can be successfully modified using powdered artificial sweetener, and people with diabetes would be fine if they had a smaller serve. Monitoring blood sugar levels also provides feedback to the amounts suitable for you.

Which artificial sweetener is best? Some recipes can be made with powdered artificial sweetener formulated to replace sugar on a spoon-for-spoon, cup-for-cup measurement basis. (Note that not all powdered artificial sweeteners are suitable in baking because some of them break down in temperature extremes and lose their effectiveness, for example, Equal.) A liquid artificial sweetener may not give the same results.

Why do some recipes state "Additional carbohydrate required"? Some recipes contain very little carbohydrate. Carbohydrate foods keep your energy reserves and blood glucose levels topped up, and it's especially important for people with diabetes to have carbohydrate with every meal. Therefore, additional carbohydrate foods need to be included with the recipe.

Which carbohydrate foods are best? The best foods are nutritious carbohydrate foods that are low in fat and/or high in fibre such as breads, breakfast cereals, rice and other grains, pasta, legumes, corn, potato and sweet potato, fruit, low-fat milk and yogurt. Limit added fats with these foods, such as spreads on bread, margarine on potatoes and cream sauces with pasta. Carbohydrate foods should be eaten in amounts that satisfy your appetite. Specific amounts are best recommended by a dietitian who can assess your individual needs.

How often is "occasional use"? All foods can be enjoyed by people with diabetes. Some foods can be eaten daily, while others are best enjoyed occasionally. Monitoring your blood sugar levels and weight provides feedback to the frequency and amounts of food suitable for you.

Why do I need fibre? You need 30 to 40 grams per day. Fibre is mother nature's way of satisfying your appetite. It also keeps your digestive system healthy and reduces blood fat and sugar levels.

A reminder... Everyone with diabetes is advised to see a dietitian who can then assist in designing an individualised meal plan. Diabetes Australia or the Dietitians Association of Australia in your capital city can direct you to your nearest dietitian. With the right guidance, you can enjoy food even more.

Compiled by dietitians Anne-Marie Mackintosh and Helen Mackenzie at Diabetes Australia-NSW.